EXPAN
REBELLION

MANCHESTER
1824

Manchester University Press

EXPANSION REBELLION

USING THE LAW TO FIGHT A RUNWAY AND SAVE THE PLANET

CELESTE HICKS

Manchester University Press

The right of Celeste Hicks to be identified as the author of this work has been asserted by them in accordance with the Copyright, Designs and Patents Act 1988.

Published by Manchester University Press
Oxford Road, Manchester M13 9PL
www.manchesteruniversitypress.co.uk

British Library Cataloguing-in-Publication Data
A catalogue record for this book is available from the British Library

ISBN 978 1 5261 6235 9 paperback

First published 2022

The publisher has no responsibility for the persistence or accuracy of URLs for any external or third-party internet websites referred to in this book, and does not guarantee that any content on such websites is, or will remain, accurate or appropriate.

Typeset
by Cheshire Typesetting Ltd, Cuddington, Cheshire
Printed in Great Britain
by Bell & Bain Ltd, Glasgow

CONTENTS

ACKNOWLEDGEMENTS

Sincere thanks to Joana Setzer at LSE for her interest and support from the beginning, and for ideas which took this book in directions I never imagined. To everyone at Friends of the Earth for their creativity and commitment, and to Tim Crosland for his patient explanations and answers to my innumerable legal questions. Thanks to Cait Hewitt at AEF for some invaluable introductions and sense checks, and Nic Ferriday for his long memory. Thanks to my editor at MUP, Tom Dark. And to Dave, Laurie, Ned and Rowan for love and understanding throughout.

INTRODUCTION

A small crowd had gathered outside a church community hall in Vauxhall, south London. On a hot June afternoon, a new round of public consultations on the plans to expand London's Heathrow airport, which had been approved by MPs the previous year, was beginning.

The organisers of the consultation, wearing purple T-shirts, hovered cautiously by the entrance; each member of the public who arrived was given a nervous look up and down before being allowed to enter the hall. Word had gone out that Extinction Rebellion was planning to 'swarm' the event with climate activists. The organisers weren't quite sure whether to look for crusty hippies with dreadlocks or neatly dressed old ladies. The recent protests on Waterloo Bridge had shown that the movement was significantly age-diverse; most of those attending the consultation did not look exceptional.

Inside the room, which doubles as a playgroup and a rehearsal venue for an amateur orchestra, Heathrow Airport Holdings Limited had set up a panoramic display demonstrating the scope of the plans. On one side was a map of the proposed new runway, on the other the estimated paths for the extra flights. In the centre, on a table, was a model of the proposed runway and terminal buildings, complete with miniature cars on the approach road.

The room had a steady buzz of activity. Although most Londoners associate aircraft noise with Richmond and Kingston, in recent years the problem has begun to affect a wider stretch of south-west and south-east London. Local campaign group Plane Hell says that, starting from 2016, the consolidation of flight paths on the approach to Heathrow has led to a large increase in the number of flights over Camberwell, Brixton, Clapham and Vauxhall. Many people in these areas have begun to experience disturbance from an increased number of planes coming in to land, often starting as early as 4.30am. This has been compounded by flights also coming in to approach London City Airport to the east. Many of the local residents who had turned up to the consultation were there to talk about the disturbance from aircraft noise.

In one corner, a young mum was remonstrating with a transport planner in his early twenties. He tried repeatedly to explain that, although it seemed logical that adding another runway and an extra 700 flights a day would lead to more noise, in fact this would not be so: 'the new plans will open up new areas for aircraft to fly over which will dilute the concentration over south-west London,' he said, pointing to a diagram showing how the location of the new 'north-west' runway and the prevailing winds would mean that a significant proportion of the air traffic would be diverted further north. 'So, you see, there will actually be *fewer* flights coming in over this part of south-east London,' he said, hopefully.

'But I don't want you to displace the flights from me only to make it worse for other people who don't already have to deal with this nuisance!' retorted the mum. 'And whatever you say, I don't believe you. I'm up every night with my young children, and I can tell you almost every day those planes start coming in at 4.30am.'

'Yes, yes, that's because of the congestion … that's why we need to have another runway, so that we don't have delayed planes backing up all day,' replied the planner, slightly exasperated. 'We could have a longer respite break overnight and start arrivals later …'

As the debate continued, there was a loud drumbeat outside the hall. And then another. All the conversation dwindled to a low murmur; the representatives of Heathrow Airport looked at each other nervously.

In the street outside, the Extinction Rebellion swarm was arriving on bikes. Ringing bells and waving brightly coloured flags, about thirty activists rode up to the door. The caretaker of the building pulled aside the organiser of the consultation, concerned about potential damage to the church hall. The activists were smiling and joking, and walked straight into the hall through the open door. Once inside they banged the drum again, and one of them stood up to make a speech. It was short. 'We are Extinction Rebellion. We disagree with the plans to expand Heathrow Airport at a time of climate emergency. To demonstrate the fears that we have for the impact of this project, we're going to hold a die-in.'

At that point, the activists lay down on the stone floor of the church hall and closed their eyes. The remaining members of the public and the organisers looked on, uncertain. There was almost complete silence. A couple of people stretched and moved their arms, but stayed lying on the floor. No-one quite knew what to expect.

After about five minutes, they all stood up. The organiser said 'Thank you', and they all went out of the front door. The church caretaker hastily locked the door behind them and informed the organisers that the event was closed. Members of the public were asked to leave. People moved slowly into the late summer's evening.

Heathrow expansion has been like a zombie. On several occasions since the 2000s the idea has raised its head, been beaten down and apparently killed off, only to resurface in a different form a few years later. In 2010, it looked as if the plans had been finished off for good, but then in 2014 plans for a third runway were relaunched by the coalition government. In 2018 Parliament controversially voted by a large majority to approve the plan for a new north-west runway, a decision which caused outcry among environmentalists and in communities that lie under the flight path.

This showdown in a run-down south London church hall in June 2019 may have seemed just the latest in a long line of conflicts between those who argue that expanding the airport is essential for Britain's global competitiveness and job creation, and those who argue that their lives are being blighted by an endless increase in noise, pollution and disturbance. But this time round the context has changed. The stakes are much higher. Over the twenty years of disagreement over expansion, the impacts of climate change have moved from being the stuff of dystopian future fiction to a clear reality that many people experience in their daily lives. Forest fires, melting ice, changing weather patterns, some of the hottest years on record have all occurred in the last ten years. Although global progress on limiting emissions over those twenty years has very little to show, the UK's climate ambition at least has steadily increased. In 2008, Britain introduced the world's first legally binding emissions reduction targets in the Climate Change Act, which committed to an 80% cut in emissions of greenhouse gases (GHG), from 1990 levels, by 2050. In 2015, the UK signed the Paris Agreement on climate change along with 195 other countries, breaking a twenty-year deadlock over the responsibility for climate leadership. Although this document did not commit any country to legally binding reductions targets, it did include the radical statement that the international community should do what it could to keep global temperature rises to within 1.5°C above pre-industrial times. Before 2015, 1.5°C had been seen as an outsider position, with ambition focused on the easier-to-achieve 2°C limit. In 2018, a seminal report from the Inter-governmental Panel on Climate Change (IPCC) starkly set out the difference between those two figures. Under a 1.5°C scenario, 6% of the world's insects would be lost; under a 2°C scenario that figure rises to 18%. Under a 2°C scenario, almost all coral reefs would bleach and die. Under a 1.5°C scenario, 14% of the world's population would be exposed to extreme heat every five years, under 2°C that figure rises to 37%.

The Paris Agreement obliges countries to submit nationally determined contributions (NDCs), which are national climate plans which highlight targets and policies governments will implement as their contribution to the global effort to reduce emissions. Overall, signatory countries are committed to achieving Net Zero GHG emissions – or a balance between emissions and carbon removals (forests, peatlands and experimental technologies, etc.) – by the middle of the twenty-first century if the 1.5°C limit is to be achieved. In practice this means each country examining every sector of its economy and designing policies in line with this goal. Energy generation, transportation, agriculture, waste management and all the rest must be set on a path to Net Zero emissions.

Throughout these discussions, flying has been seen as something of a special case. International aviation was not covered by the Paris Agreement, nor was it in the original UK Climate Change Act as passed in 2008. This is largely because aviation is viewed as a hard-to-treat sector, and until relatively recently was making a small contribution to global GHG emissions. The enormous amounts of energy required to get a plane airborne and keep it there mean that attempts to find a credible alternative to kerosene are far behind the development of alternative forms of electrically propelled vehicles (EVs). Another sticking point is that there have long been disagreements about where to treat the emissions from international aviation as arising – should accounting be based on the country from which the plane departs, where it lands, the nationality of the passenger(s) or the country where the airline is registered? Aviation is also difficult to quantify because it has additional 'non-CO2' impacts on climate, which come from the release of other gases such as sulphur dioxide, nitrogen oxide and water vapour. These gases have complex chemical interactions higher up in the atmosphere. There is some dispute about how long these effects last for and how they interplay, but there is a general agreement that they more or less double the CO2 impacts alone. Nevertheless, some scientific uncertainty over the scale of the impacts has delayed efforts at mitigation.

But while attempts to address aviation emissions have stalled over the last twenty years and there are few clear laws on emissions from the sector in the UK, global aviation itself has exploded. Until the coronavirus pandemic hit in early 2020, the sector represented one of the fastest growing emitters of GHGs. By 2019 aircraft carbon emissions had more than doubled across the EU since 1990. Passenger numbers have doubled since the early 1990s. Department for Transport projections see those numbers increasing by another 64% by 2050. And aviation is a highly carbon-intensive sector. One person taking a return flight from London to Edinburgh has a larger carbon footprint than does the average person in Uganda in the course of a whole year.[1] While other sectors of the economy such as electricity generation are undergoing dramatic decarbonisation, aviation has not been required to make those cuts.

All of this comes before the proposed expansion of the UK's largest airport, Heathrow, is taken into account. In its plans for a third runway, Heathrow Airport hoped to increase passenger numbers passing through its terminals by some 70% by 2050. Modelling suggested that this would involve an extra 700 planes *per day* arriving at one of the world's most congested sites, an additional 260,000 flights per year.[2]

The debates raging over the merits of expanding Heathrow occurred at a period when two powerful social protest movements emerged, during the latter part of 2018 – Fridays for Future (or Youth Strike for Climate) inspired by the Swedish teenager Greta Thunberg, and Extinction Rebellion. Both of these groups denounced the climate record of the UK government. They argued that, although the UK has good laws and strives to be a climate leader, progress on actually reducing carbon emissions has been poor. The Commons vote to allow expansion at Heathrow to proceed happened just as these movements were gathering momentum. The apparent hypocrisy of approving a third runway for one of the world's biggest airports at a time that the UK government was claiming to be a global climate leader was not hard to see.

It is worth pausing for a moment to reflect on the scale of the change in the climate change policy landscape since 2018. When, that year, the House of Commons voted to approve Heathrow expansion, the UK's target was to reduce GHG emissions by 80% from 1990 levels by 2050 (established in the 2008 Climate Change Act). The UK was already on course to meet its interim target, a 35% reduction by 2020. But just a year later, in June 2019, the government committed to reaching Net Zero by 2050. This was a very significant change.

One legal case served to bring all that into focus. On 1 May 2019 – the very day that Parliament declared a climate emergency largely in response to the demands of the Extinction Rebellion and Youth Strike for Climate protestors – the High Court threw out a legal challenge that had tried to stop Heathrow expansion in its tracks. The timing of the decision was awful. The challenge was the first time in the UK that a case had been based on the state's responsibilities under the 2015 Paris Agreement. One of the fundamental questions at the heart of the case was whether it was acceptable to hand over to an expanded airport what remained of the UK's overall 'carbon budget' – essentially the quantity of greenhouse gases the UK can emit and still keep temperatures below that 1.5°C limit. The judicial review into the designation of the Airports National Policy Statement (ANPS) happened at a time that the ground was shifting, and the case became a symbol that defined that era.

You may have heard about the Heathrow expansion plans, and like many others been confused by the tortuous back and forth over the last twenty years. There have been many U-turns; at times it seemed that the third runway was a certainty, at others a lunacy. You may have also heard about this legal challenge (which I will call the Heathrow judicial review or JR), and in particular the spectacular victory in February 2020 when the Court of Appeal ruled that the government's own policy on airport expansion *was* in fact illegal, seeming to consign the expansion plans to history. Ten months later, in the middle of a pandemic which had seen the global airline industry faced with unprecedented changes in global travelling behaviour, a final Supreme Court victory reinstated that policy and seemed to pave the way for a new runway, a decision which seemed to many campaigners to be hopelessly out of step with the fundamental changes to the UK's climate commitments that had occurred in the intervening years.

This book will trace the, at times, radical shifts in public awareness of the climate crisis and government responses to it which have occurred in the last three years. The story is not yet over, and there is much space yet to be contested, but this book will argue that with the Heathrow JR the genie is out of the bottle. Win or lose, this case was a highly symbolic victory in the battle to hold politicians to account for making promises to decarbonise. It clearly showed the gap between political rhetoric and the substance of assessing the carbon impacts of new national infrastructure projects, a gap which is only widening as global emissions continue to rise. This case was the first in a process of establishing what the Paris Agreement actually means in domestic law. Other cases were inspired and influenced by it – at least four other significant judicial reviews of large infrastructure programmes were launched around the same time and on similar grounds to the Heathrow case.

Those who bring these cases are fed up with hypocrisy. They are no longer willing to have politicians sign international and domestic laws which commit us to ambitious decarbonisation targets on one hand, while simultaneously creating policies which will have the opposite effect.

This book is the story of how that ground-breaking Heathrow legal challenge was constructed. It will look at how this strategic climate litigation came about in the unfolding *zeitgeist* of growing public concern on climate change. Crucially, it will examine how the impacts of the case go well beyond the future of just one airport, and touch upon the urgency of ensuring that all our future national infrastructure projects are conceived with significant carbon reductions in mind.

Reports of the death of Heathrow are exaggerated

As this book will show, the significant win at the appeals court in February 2020 was not the first time campaigners had claimed victory in the battle against Heathrow expansion. The euphoria was short-lived and by the end of the year the Supreme Court ruled in favour of Heathrow Airport, paving the way for them to submit an application for a development consent order (DCO) covering the expansion plans. Even though the CEO of Heathrow, John Holland-Kaye, has said publicly that the new runway may not be needed for ten years due to the collapse in demand following the coronavirus pandemic, if a DCO is granted it will leave the airport free to develop the runway whenever it sees fit. This story could run and run as the climate warms.

This book will examine the sheer size of the estimated £17bn plan to build a north-west runway at Heathrow, which involves digging a tunnel, rerouting the M25 to run through it, diverting several rivers, knocking down 700 homes and rebuilding a swathe of road infrastructure. It will examine the at times controversial economic projections which were used by the independent body that recommended the third runway as the preferred option for the government's aviation planning document, the ANPS. Two different forecasts were used – at one end of the scale an estimate that the new runway would generate a £147bn bounty for the UK economy, at the other a mere £1bn in benefits over sixty years. The book will explore the potential for increased carbon emissions from a third runway and the 700 extra flights daily, and how that might impact on the UK's commitments to achieve Net Zero GHG emissions by 2050.

In some ways this story is just about one airport and one runway. For the proponents of expansion, it has been argued that an expanded Heathrow's contribution to rising global emissions is inconsequential. Previous battles against Heathrow expansion have been presented as local NIMBY issues – just a small group of west Londoners bothered by the constant howl of jet engines above their houses. However, the real power of this story is that, this time round, the legal challenge hit a profound change in the public understanding of climate change and became a *national* issue. The Heathrow JR succeeded in showing that in the battle to keep global temperatures to 1.5°C above pre-industrial levels every new infrastructure project in every country of the world matters. Leaders cannot simply say one thing and do another. The Court of Appeal victory in February 2020 had an important influence on four other challenges going through the courts at around that time, including against the UK's energy policy and a £27bn roads investment plan. I argue that these challenges have one thing in common – they represent a radical and symbolic attempt by individuals to say enough is enough. We cannot keep on building carbon-intensive infrastructure. This is no longer about the future; the cuts we need to see in GHG emissions need to be made now. It is in our lifetime, perhaps within the next decade, that we will know whether we have done enough to hold temperatures to what the international community aspired to in Paris in 2015, a rise of no more than 1.5°C.

Chapter 1 looks at the history of the legal frameworks which formed the grounds for the Heathrow JR. This includes the 2008 Planning Act – which paved the way for the new National Policy Statements (NPS) on nationally significant infrastructure, but also placed requirements to ensure that these developments were sustainable – and of course the UK's flagship 2008 Climate Change Act which was the first piece of legislation anywhere in the world to place legally binding emissions reductions targets on a country. It will also examine the lead up to the 2015 Paris Agreement on Climate Change, explaining how the document navigated the top-down versus bottom-up approaches to tackling climate change and issues of differentiated responsibility for climate change between different nations. Chapter 2 looks at the plans to expand Heathrow, including a detailed examination of the designation of the ANPS in 2018. It examines the economic arguments put forward in favour of expansion, including the cost of abating the carbon impacts of the project, and looks at what impact the development would have on the ground in west London. Chapter 3 tells the story of the Heathrow JR, with first-hand testimony from the key legal figures involved in developing the challenge. It looks at how the case was developed against a background of unprecedented interest and concern over the climate crisis inspired by Extinction Rebellion and Fridays for Future. Chapter 4 evaluates some of the options for decarbonising aviation and examines the recommendations of the government's independent advisors on climate change. Chapter 5 examines the aftermath of the Heathrow JR and attempts to situate the judgment in the context of fast-evolving strategic climate litigation. It also looks at what the coronavirus pandemic might mean for global aviation, and whether the business case for Heathrow expansion still stands up. Finally, it examines how the UK government's ambition to be a climate leader in the run-up to the CoP26 climate change summit in Glasgow in late 2021 led it to make increasingly ambitious GHG emissions reduction targets.

1

BUILDING THE UK'S CLIMATE CHANGE FRAMEWORK

It is no overstatement to say that the Judicial Review into the plans to expand Heathrow Airport under the Airports National Policy Statement in March 2019 was as ambitious as the plan to expand the airport itself. Four separate claims with twenty-two subclauses were 'rolled up' into one hearing which lasted ten days. Reams of background material were generated for the two judges, Lord Justice Hickinbottom and Mr Justice Holgate. So great was the interest from media, supporters and the public that the case was heard in the largest room at the Royal Courts of Justice, and an extra room with a TV link was prepared in the expectation of an overspill. The case drew on an immense background of environmental and planning law, both domestic and international, stretching back more than twelve years.

This chapter will seek to lay out the legal frameworks which underpinned the first ever case in the UK which sought to uphold commitments made under the Paris Agreement. It will also outline the startlingly fast changes in the UK government's climate ambition which took place from 2018–19, in part inspired by the commitments which it had entered into under the Paris Agreement.

The Paris Agreement on climate change

Climate change, or global warming as it was first called, is a global problem. No one country can deal with it alone. Humans have known about the dangers of releasing large amounts of carbon dioxide into the atmosphere for a long time. Scientists first began to study the carbon cycle in the late nineteenth century. Their work began the process of understanding the Earth's natural processes that move carbon into and out of the atmosphere to be sequestered in the soil, oceans and deep underground; they began to study the natural 'greenhouse effect' and the changes that had led the Earth in and out of Ice Ages. They began to speculate that emitting large quantities of CO_2 into the atmosphere would trap solar radiation, leading to global warming. As the fossil fuel age accelerated, they began to understand that digging up and burning the coal, oil and natural gas that had been stored away effectively releases millions of years of solar energy which had previously been removed from the atmosphere. In 1988 NASA scientist James Hansen presented evidence to the US Congress of the relationship between burning fossil fuels and the accumulation of carbon dioxide in the atmosphere. His work had been influenced by his study into the atmosphere of Venus, where scientists suspected that runaway climate change billions of years ago had turned its atmosphere into a toxic cloud of sulphur dioxide.

At first there was some optimism that global agreement on tackling anthropogenic climate change could be found. The Montreal Protocol on the release of chlorofluorocarbon (CFC) gases was signed by almost all countries in 1987, leading to quick action to limit the use of CFCs and an attempt to fix the hole in the ozone layer. The Protocol's format of a top-down agreement phasing out the production and consumption of ozone-depleting substances was seen as the golden formula for reaching international consensus on environmental protection efforts. Another environmental disaster – acid rain caused by the emission of sulphur dioxide and nitrogen oxides from industrial processes and road traffic – had been discovered in 1963, and by the late 1980s action to tackle the worst aspects of that pollution was ramping up.

In 1992, the greenhouse effect problem came to wide global attention with the Rio Earth summit in Brazil. At the summit, 107 heads of state agreed the establishment of the United Nations Framework Convention on Climate Change (UNFCCC). The agreement set no limits on emissions, but instead established a framework for future negotiations on reducing greenhouse gas emissions. Participating countries would meet to discuss targets, strategies for reduction and progress at an annual Conference of Parties (CoP), an event which continues today with CoP26 (the twenty-sixth meeting) being held in the UK in late 2021. Early progress on agreeing reductions looked promising – in 1997 the Kyoto Protocol was agreed at CoP3 in Japan. This was the first time countries agreed to legally mandated, country-specific emissions reductions. However, these reductions were modest and only applied to developed countries – essentially industrialised economies including Western countries, members of the Organisation for Economic Co-operation and Development and some countries from Europe's former Eastern bloc. These forty-three countries became known as 'Annex 1' countries. This onus on developed countries to lead the action arose because, early in the process, the concept that climate change was inequitable began to emerge. Global temperatures were rising on the back of 150 years of rich countries burning fossil fuels, which had allowed them to make astounding economic development gains, while poorer countries had hardly begun their economic transitions. Many of these less developed countries, notably India and China, argued successfully that they should not be required to scale back the use of fossil fuels if this meant being unable to develop and grow their economies to a standard equivalent to the biggest polluters.

This inequity issue, and the ineffective strategies used to tackle it, became a significant block on effective climate change mitigation during the 2000s. The lack of restrictions on India and China was a large factor behind the US refusal to ratify Kyoto, and the legacy of those arguments is still apparent today. It took seven years for the Kyoto Protocol to come into legal effect (in 2005), partly because many new rules and processes had to be developed. But by then India and China's rapid development and consequent increased use of fossil fuels meant that the Protocol's impact was limited. The document failed to curtail rising emissions and led some to speculate that international negotiations had reached a dead end. By 2007, China had become the world's largest emitter of CO_2, and by 2012 its total emissions equalled those of the USA and the EU combined.[1]

By the late 2000s the equity issue was becoming deeply problematic. One of the true low points in climate action occurred at the CoP15 summit in Copenhagen in 2009. In the months leading up to the talks, observers became increasingly concerned that a workable text for a Conference agreement would not be achievable, largely because political will to 'engage in real negotiations' was lacking.[2] When world leaders arrived for the final stages of the conference in the Danish capital there was no real draft text to agree. The Danish hosts of the conference allowed the negotiations to split informally into two blocks – one contained the USA, the BASIC countries (Brazil, South Africa, India and China) and 'Friends of the Chair', and the other covered the rest of the world. US President Obama, fearful of being unable to get any deal past domestic opponents in the pro-business Senate, was accused of rebuking China to conceal his own lack of ambition. The deal that eventually emerged was agreed behind closed doors and appeared to lock out poorer nations and those which would be most vulnerable to the effects of climate change. As a sweetener, Obama pushed for commitments towards $100bn per year in climate finance, to help developing nations adapt. Another small success was a move away from the old distinction between Annex 1 and non-Annex countries, opening up space for negotiation in future years. Nevertheless, the final text has been heavily criticised. Smaller nations were forced to accept the deal, which was vague about the commitment to keep global temperatures below 2°C and failed to demand binding emissions cuts from any country. They were left feeling abandoned and shut out of what should have been a global accord. 'You only have to see some of the South American bodyguards skittling bystanders in the crowded conference foyer to know these are men who expect to be centre stage, not watching pay-per-view in the hotel room,' said the BBC's environment correspondent Roger Harrabin.[3] The talks were largely regarded as a failure.

Bad CoP, good CoP

In the aftermath of the Copenhagen conference, there were fears that global climate policy could now become confined to the actions of a small, self-appointed group of powerful nations. However, just one year later, at CoP16 in Cancun, things started to look more hopeful. This conference produced meaningful conclusions on what was meant by adaptation, or finance flows to help countries which suffer the greatest impacts from climate change. It also adopted 'below 2°C' as a temperature goal, and launched a process of periodic review of whether this long-term goal would be adequate. This would become critical when, in 2018, the IPCC published its seminal report into the importance of keeping global temperature rises to 1.5°C.

Realising the scale of the *impasse* which had been created by this inability to find a fair burden-sharing arrangement, the 2011 CoP17 in Durban, South Africa, began the process of moving the world towards another globally binding treaty to replace Kyoto by 2020. The conference agreed that a new treaty would require all the countries not included in Kyoto – notably the USA, India and China – to reduce their emissions. 'Copenhagen will have redeemed itself if it will have served as the final wake-up call for our collective leadership,' argued Benito Müller of the Oxford Institute for Energy Studies.[4]

At subsequent CoPs in Warsaw (2013) and Lima (2014) the idea of increasing ambition for emissions reductions became popular. 'The narrative was beginning to change from ambition as a major cost to economies ... to one of abundant opportunity that could be unlocked through practical international co-operation.'[5] It also began to shift towards a more consensual approach, away from formal commitments towards informal ambition driven through working together; more carrot, less stick. This was the beginning of the concept of the 'intended nationally determined contribution' (INDC), or voluntary pledge to cut emissions put forward by a national government. This allowed countries to set their own ambition and would become the keystone of the Paris Agreement.

CoP20 in Paris 2015

The Le Bourget conference centre outside Paris was built on an airfield where Charles Lindbergh had landed after his famous first flight across the Atlantic. When the delegates finally arrived in December 2015 there was a palpable sense of hope. Security was tight in the aftermath of terrorist attacks just a week earlier at the Bataclan nightclub, in which 130 people had died, but nevertheless the conference went ahead. Negotiations during the previous year had focused on moving the draft text to a more workable place, and the French hosts had spent many diplomatic hours behind the scenes.

This time round the negotiators seemed better prepared to unlock the controversial problems of what had become known as 'differentiation' – essentially how much action should be assigned to individual countries according to their own historical and current responsibility for emissions. Lessons had been learned from the Annex 1 divisions of Kyoto, and now China was far and away the biggest polluter, action had to be global with all countries making mitigation pledges. The onus seemed to be tipping towards voluntary contributions with the hope that collective action would inspire better results; an effort to 'break the 15-year logjam ... by radically restructuring the game ... from one in which bad actors are punished by economic penalties, to one of voluntary pledges in which bad actors are shamed'.[6] The big industrial nations seemed to be more aware that real commitments on financing adaptation and damages for loss suffered through climate-related disasters would have to be forthcoming.

Significantly, during the last few days of the conference a 'High Ambition Coalition' (HAC) emerged as a growing force. The group, which had been formed in secret six months before the conference, included seventy-nine African, Caribbean and Pacific nations, the USA and all of the EU member states. The coalition, led by the foreign minister of the vulnerable Marshall Islands Tony de Brun, had four clear goals: an agreement at Paris to be legally binding; to set a clear long-term goal on global warming in line with scientific advice; to introduce a mechanism for reviewing countries' emissions commitments every five years; and to create a unified system for tracking countries' progress on meeting their carbon goals.[7]

The HAC succeeded in achieving some of its goals. The most important for the future debates over the compatibility of plans to expand Heathrow Airport with achieving emissions reductions, was that the final text of Paris included the phrase 'efforts to limit the temperature increase to 1.5°C above pre-industrial levels'. In a '1.5 to stay alive' campaign many of the countries more vulnerable to climate change, such as African nations and small island states, had been arguing for 1.5°C to be the limit since 2009. However, inclusion of this temperature goal 'was far from a foregone conclusion',[8] even at the beginning of the Paris conference. With support from non-government organisations (NGOs) and campaign groups, the HAC was critical in securing this concession. The purpose of the goal is to limit the risks and impacts of climate change through ensuring that CO_2 emissions reach a global peak, and that rapid decarbonisation begins, as soon as possible. It was a major victory for the HAC and vulnerable countries. To further consolidate the efforts towards 1.5°C, the IPCC was asked to produce a detailed report (to be presented in 2018) into the difference in impact globally if the temperature rise was limited to 1.5°C, rather than 2°C. I will turn to that report later.

Paris also succeeded in establishing a mechanism to review progress on emissions cuts every five years. Negotiators were keen to privilege sovereignty and respect national circumstances, which led to the development of the concept of NDCs. However, it became clear early on that the sum of the INDCs submitted before the Paris conference would miss the 2°C goal, never mind the 1.5°C goal, by a considerable margin. The response was to build a cycle of increasing ambition into the deal, which became known as 'ratcheting' of commitments. There was an initial commitment to no backsliding, and the final text included provisions to ensure increasing ambition through the use of the global stocktake. This is essentially a commitment to review progress every five years; the first review is due to take place in 2023, with a view to increasing ambition once initial goals have been met. This is one of the few top-down measures in the whole agreement, but the emphasis is on tracking collective progress rather than singling out any nation for failing to meet its engagements.

Seven years on from the Paris Agreement, this voluntary commitment recognising the crucial role of domestic politics is still being tested and clarified. Interestingly for this story, this approach contrasts with the 'top-down' approach of the UK's Climate Change Act 2008 (CCA 08), which obliges the country to meet legally binding reduction targets.

The agreement established that Net Zero would need to be achieved globally by 2050. Net Zero has become a widespread term, but a common usage only emerged in the last few years.

The term means achieving a balance between the volume of GHGs emitted into the atmosphere and the volume removed from it. The balance – or net zero – will be struck when the amount of carbon added to the atmosphere every year no longer exceeds the amount that is removed. There are two ways to remove carbon from the atmosphere. The first is through natural processes, the most significant of which are photosynthesis – trees and vegetation absorbing CO_2 – and the oceans – plankton and algae use about 25% of the carbon currently emitted as CO_2 and then die, drawing it to the seabed. The other way is through engineered removals or technology. Net Zero cannot be achieved using only these processes – emissions need to fall dramatically as well. Natural processes take time to remove the carbon; for example it takes many years for trees to mature sufficiently to absorb large amounts of carbon and we cannot be sure that the forests will still be there in fifty years. Secondly, many of the technologies which have been proposed are still in their infancy, so it will take many years for them to be deployed at scale, even as we continue to emit increasing amounts of GHGs every year. Technology and natural processes will also be required to remove the excess CO_2 which is *already* in the atmosphere and *already* causing extreme weather.

Two technologies which the UK's Climate Change Committee (CCC) believes hold promise are BECCS (bio energy with carbon capture and storage) and DACCS (direct air carbon capture and storage). BECCS essentially means burning biomass for energy and sequestering the carbon which is released, and DACCS means removing CO_2 directly from the air. In both cases the CO_2 is compressed into a liquid and taken away for permanent storage. But we need to allow time for these technologies to be developed. We still need to reduce emissions dramatically while we wait for this to happen; eventually emissions need to be reduced to as near actual zero as can be managed so these technologies can start removing CO_2.

There are still no guarantees that the worst dangers from climate change can be avoided. Some have called the Paris Agreement a 'transformational' document, but the question is 'whether it provides a robust yet adaptable framework for developing and sustaining long-term political commitment to an effective global response'.[9] In 2019, the CCC estimated that if Net Zero is achieved globally by 2050, there would be a greater than 50% chance of limiting temperature rises to 1.5°C by 2100. These are not great odds, but even in that scenario, carbon would still need to be removed from the atmosphere for years to come, achieving a net negative carbon balance and restoring global CO_2 concentrations in the atmosphere to a stable pre-industrial level of around 280 parts per million (ppm).

The UK's Climate Change Act

Interestingly, the Heathrow JR and other similar cases seeking to uphold emissions reduction commitments made by the UK government have not relied on the UK's seminal Climate Change Act, passed in October 2008. This was the first law anywhere in the world to place a legally binding, long-term, emissions reduction target on a government in order to combat climate change. The new law obliged the UK to reduce its greenhouse gas emissions by 80% from 1990 levels by 2050, and it was passed a full seven years before the Net Zero 2050 targets were discussed at CoP20 in 2015.

There were a number of reasons why the campaigners chose not to use the CCA 08 in the Heathrow JR. As a baseline document, the CCA 08 had already set ambitious reductions targets, which were strengthened to Net Zero in 2019. It was hard to argue in court that the targets in themselves are insufficient. In addition, when the claim in the Heathrow JR was being drawn up, international aviation emissions were still not formally included in the CCA 08 targets; and because the Act covers the whole UK economy it has been argued that it is hard to show that one particular sector or project would single-handedly exhaust the carbon budget. So why does the CCA 08 matter for this story? In fact, the Act came to play an important role in the courtroom debate about the importance of the Paris Agreement in UK law. In the final judgment on the Heathrow JR case in December 2020, the Supreme Court established that the CCA 08 is the correct piece of legislation against which to assess the climate impacts of future infrastructure projects.

The CCA 08 was the culmination of a concerted campaign from civil society groups, in particular Friends of the Earth (FoE) and its 'Big Ask' campaign. These groups felt frustrated that previous attempts by the UK government to tackle climate change had seen little real progress. The Big Ask campaign was conceived in 2004, when the government's scientific advisor David King warned that global greenhouse emissions should be stabilised at 450ppm instead of 550ppm, a previous limit. At that time the UK appeared to have achieved its modest Kyoto targets as a largely unintended consequence of the shift away from coal-powered electricity generation in the 1990s, but deeper emissions cuts were looking elusive. As a policy issue, climate change was not a major concern in the later days of the Blair administration.

The idea for the campaign emerged from an 'ad hoc conversation in a stairwell' at the FoE offices in London in 2004.

Bryony Worthington (now Baroness Worthington) and political campaigner Martyn Williams discussed the idea of creating a UK 'carbon budget' which would reflect the aim of achieving binding emissions cuts agreed at Kyoto.

> I was into the numbers of climate change so I was tracking the annual emissions and saw that there was just no trend any more, whereas they'd been falling steadily in the 1990s, from 1997 onwards it started to just bounce around and there was no discernible trend down, and yet we had these glossy strategies that were supposed to be doing something about it. So I just got very frustrated and said we've got to change the way we do this [said Worthington].[10]

She took part in FoE's official response to the government's climate review, and made the case for a top-down approach, setting overall emission reduction targets for individual economic sectors. This concept became known as a carbon budget, which means setting an overall limit to the amount of CO_2 which can be emitted if the UK, and ultimately the world, is to manage to keep below a temperature threshold. Worthington and Williams felt that this should be a legal requirement, which meant that if the budget was exceeded there should be a legal route to recourse. It should not really matter to what extent individual sectors decarbonised, as long as emissions reductions were balanced across the economy, and overall they fell. It was up to politicians to decide which sectors could go further faster and which ones should be permitted to take longer to decarbonise.

Friends of the Earth came up with the idea of writing a draft bill, and asking supporters to contact their local MP to ask them to support it. It was something that individual people and communities could engage in, and offered them a simple, practical step. FoE called on the government to legally commit to reducing total carbon dioxide emissions by 3% year-on-year, which would add up to an 80% reduction by 2050. It was a 'coherent, positive and impassioned pro-climate action message', argues Thomas Muinzer, 'which combined a media strategy, public events and the burgeoning use of internet tactics to create a grassroots movement calling for change'.[11]

The campaign was fronted by Thom Yorke, the singer from Radiohead, actor Gillian Anderson, Stephen Fry and Helen Baxendale. In 2005, the model Climate Bill was introduced in the House of Commons by a group of cross-bench MPs – John Gummer (Conservative), Michael Meacher (Labour) and Norman Baker (Liberal Democrats). David Cameron had been elected leader of the Conservative party in 2005, and quickly latched onto the idea of using the environment as a way to detoxify the image of the Conservatives as the nasty party. In May 2006, Thom Yorke and Jonny Greenwood played a Big Ask concert in London.

Later that year, the influential Stern Report clarified the economic case for investing in national decarbonisation. The idea of carbon budgeting seemed to appeal to the business community, as it offered the prospect of locking in a degree of market certainty and stability over time. In the end, more than 200,000 people contacted their MPs. Over 400 MPs signed up to back the creation of a bill, and significantly David Cameron, leader of the Opposition, was an early backer. 'What emerged was an unprecedented cross-party "competitive consensus" involving all three major parties trying to "out-green" each other on climate change and the environment.'[12] In November 2006, the government finally announced a climate bill in the Queen's speech.

Bryony Worthington was seconded to the Department for Environment, Food & Rural Affairs (DEFRA) to help draw up the legislation. The campaign continued to push the government for an 80% reduction in place of the proposed 60%. At one point, campaigners hoped to include international aviation in the carbon budgets but, according to Worthington, it was felt that it was more important to focus on getting results from the sectors responsible for the largest emissions.[13] Crucially, FoE avoided pushing any recommendations on *how* emission cuts might be achieved, instead focusing on the principle of carbon budgets. This meant politicians had to provide the policy. 'The campaign focus on lobbying individual MPs neatly combined FoE's traditional capacity for mobilizing its grassroots activists and the wider public with a more traditional insider strategy carried out to great effect by parliamentary lobbyists working at the centre.'[14]

The law was finally passed in October 2008, with 463 MPs voting in favour. It had been shepherded through its final stages by Ed Miliband, who had recently been promoted to Secretary of State in the newly created Department for Energy and Climate Change. The 80% reduction target survived in the final draft, but emissions from international aviation and shipping were left out, to be quantified at a later stage pending further research.

When the Act was passed, the overall objective was to achieve a 34% reduction from 1990 levels of GHG emissions by 2020 (revised up from 26%), and then a further target of an 80% reduction by 2050. This target was revised to Net Zero in 2019, as I will explain later. The use of 1990 as a baseline reflected the 1996 Kyoto Protocol targets. In order to reach that long-term target, five-year carbon budgets were created for each sector of the economy – essentially an overall limit to CO_2 emissions for that period which must not be exceeded. These budgets would become steadily more ambitious over time. The first covered the period 2008–12 and required a 23% reduction from 1990 levels.

Part 2 of the CCA 2008 created a new statutory advisory body, the Committee on Climate Change (CCC – now the Climate Change Committee). The purpose of the CCC is to provide technical and scientific advice to the government about how to achieve its commitments on mitigation and adaptation and produce regular reports to Parliament about the UK's progress on decarbonisation. When the CCA 08 was drafted, it was thought that an independent, technocratic body would be more effective at taking the long-term view than politicians. The CCC also recommends carbon budgets every five years – an overall budget and detailed summaries for each individual economic sector. These are then tallied together to create an overall allowance. The budgets are set twelve years in advance to allow predictability for investors. The CCC presents these suggested budgets to Parliament which then votes on whether to approve them. Importantly for the purposes of this book, until 2021 international aviation and shipping (IAS) were not included in the carbon budgets because the decision had been made to address them at a later date. The formula instead was to leave 'head-room', or an assumed level of emissions based on real levels, when calculating the budgets for other sectors.

The CCC is an independent body whose members are scientists, economists and former politicians, appointed by the environment minister for their technical knowledge.[15] Its current chair is Lord Deben (John Gummer, who was the longest serving UK environment minister in the Conservative governments of the 1990s). The CCC's £3.7m annual budget is provided by government, and responsibility lies with DEFRA and the Department for Business, Energy and Industrial Strategy (BEIS). The government must set out the measures it will take to achieve the carbon budget requirements when it sets them into law, but it does not have to follow the CCC's recommendations. The CCC produces annual reports for Parliament about the progress made on reducing emissions. It has been argued that the CCC has been an important contributor to decoupling the UK's economic activity from GHG emissions, with 2019 figures showing that emissions had fallen 29% since 2010 (emissions reductions for 2020 were even more dramatic, following the coronavirus pandemic).[16] Through taking a long-term perspective and assisting evidence-based policymaking, it has helped to develop the credibility of carbon budgets. Nevertheless, the CCC has no legal power to overrule the government. It relies more on political embarrassment, such as revealing the gap between what has been promised and what has actually been achieved. As we shall see in the debate over whether airport expansion could be reconciled with emissions reductions, the CCC's early cautious (and polite!) attempts to challenge government policy on airport expansion were largely rebuffed.

Planning Act 2008

Despite the apparent strength of the CCA 08, it was on the basis of the more mundane Planning Act 2008 that the Heathrow JR legal teams built their case. Friends of the Earth and Plan B lawyers relied heavily on the Act's sustainable development and mitigating climate change provisions in constructing their cases. Their main line of argument was that the decision to allow future expansion at Heathrow would contravene the UK's international climate change commitments, specifically the Paris Agreement.

The Planning Act 2008 came about because, during the 2000s, the Labour government started to look at reforming the planning system. This decision was partly based on the experience of the Heathrow Terminal 5 Planning Inquiry which, when it concluded in 2000, had become the world's longest-running inquiry. The government wanted to streamline the system to deal with 'mischiefs',[17] or attempts by campaigners and lawyers to nit-pick on small points of planning law which had not been properly defined in order to stall developments. 'A key problem with the current system of planning for major infrastructure is that national policy and, in particular, the national need for infrastructure, is not in all cases clearly set out', said a White Paper published in 2007.[18] In other words, individual planning inquiries were having to decide for themselves what the national policy on infrastructure development should be, in particular contested ideas of whether the infrastructure was needed or not and how this affected developing responsibilities to deal with GHG emissions. This was particularly the case with airport expansion, and had caused significant delays in the Terminal 5 Inquiry.

The solution was a proposed system of national policy frameworks, which became known as 'National Policy Statements' (NPS). Each major sector of the economy which would need to develop infrastructure in the future would gain its own NPS – from the energy generation sector, to roads, ports and airports. The NPSs would be designated using the Planning Act as a guide which, crucially for this story, contained a number of clear provisions ensuring that the UK's climate change commitments would not be compromised. For example, section 5(8) reads 'The reasons must (in particular) include an explanation of how the policy set out in the statement takes account of Government policy relating to the mitigation of, and adaptation to, climate change'. Under the heading 'sustainable development' section 10(3a) sets the Secretary of State the objective of 'mitigating, and adapting to, climate change'.[19] This section is important and came to play a key role in the Heathrow JR ten years later. It was secured after campaigning by Friends of the Earth ahead of the Planning Act's passage in 2008. The NGO successfully established that 'the "Brundtland definition" of "sustainable development" applied: that we should "satisfy our own needs without compromising the ability of future generations to meet theirs". ... [This was] the first time Sustainable Development had been defined for the Planning Act.'[20] The Act also established an obligation to draw up an accompanying appraisal of sustainability (AoS) and a strategic environmental assessment (SEA).

A key innovation in the Planning Act was the introduction of new 'development consent orders' (DCO), which would replace the need for separate consents to be sought (compulsory purchase, planning permission, etc.). These applications would be examined by a panel of independent planning inspectors. The inspectors make a recommendation, but the final decision on granting the DCO rests with the relevant Secretary of State.[21] Once the NPSs (i.e. the national policy) had been designated under this new, more transparent procedure, the thinking was that it would be easier for developers, the public and government to see to what extent any DCO meets the requirements of the law. The Planning Act laid out a much clearer way of establishing guiding principles for what sort of future infrastructure the UK would require. The idea behind this was to avoid the legislation becoming out of date, with the assumption that technical details and changes in circumstances could be ironed out at the DCO stage.

The UK has long prided itself on this domestic legal framework for addressing climate change. The Planning Act 2008 gave a framework for assessing whether future infrastructure projects could be in line with the CCA 08 goals (reducing emissions by 80%, stabilising global temperature rises at no more than 2°C). The two pieces of legislation were passed on the same day in 2008, which twelve years later led the High Court in the Heathrow JR case to conclude that they were clearly 'meant to be read together'.[22]

Aviation peculiarity

When the Kyoto Protocol was signed in 1997, emissions from IAS were left out. At that time their significance was unclear, given how huge numbers of people in the world had never set foot in an aeroplane. Since then, aviation has fallen through the cracks of the global carbon accountability system. It was not included in the 2015 Paris Agreement, and only in 2021 did the British government finally agree to include emissions from international aviation in its sixth carbon budget stemming from CCA 08. Over that time global passenger numbers have exploded, from 1.5bn in 1997 to 4.5bn in 2018.[23] In the months before the global coronavirus pandemic hit, most industry projections were continuing to see massive growth in the industry over the coming years.

Twenty-four years after the Kyoto Protocol was signed the international plan to reduce emissions from flying remains sketchy. The UN's system for tackling aviation emissions under the auspices of the International Civil Aviation Organization (ICAO) is called CORSIA. It is low on ambition, and aims only to achieve carbon-neutral *growth* in aviation from 2020 using a system of offsetting. It does not lay out any overall emissions reduction targets for the sector. The aviation industry globally has committed to a 50% reduction by 2050 under the auspices of its trade body the International Air Transport Association (IATA), which now looks hopelessly out of step with Net Zero commitments. Some early attempts have been made to generate research and scale up the market development of sustainable aviation fuels, but the development of a commercially viable, fully electric plane for long-haul flights still seems many years away.

Meanwhile, aviation enjoys a privileged position in our economies and societies. As analyst Peter McManners argues, 'aviation is a showcase of civilisation, demonstrating human abilities to harness advanced technology to improve people's lives'.[24] Flying where we want to is part of our personal freedom. For many, there is still a sense of excitement at sitting in the window seat in order to see new lands unfolding beneath the clouds as the plane flies over them; although many jaded business travellers make the more pragmatic choice to sit in the aisle to be closer to the toilet. Flying connects people from all over the world, takes us on glamorous holidays, reunites us with long-lost family and friends and has facilitated our globalised economy. I personally flew all over the world, in particular all over Africa, in my capacity as a journalist, for the BBC and later freelance. I flew in everything from a giant Boeing to a rattling Antonov cargo plane, and in a tiny two-seater Fokker to a refugee camp in Chad. I have been through Heathrow Terminal 4 more times than I care to remember. Like many others, I would have been unable to carry out my job without being able to fly, and the privilege has opened my eyes to the complexity of the world.

However, we now know that aviation is the fastest growing source of GHG emissions, while other sectors are beginning to decarbonise rapidly. By 2018, aviation contributed about 7% of the UK's GHG emissions, and were 88% above 1990 levels.[25] In contrast, emissions from electricity generation have fallen 68% over the same period. We know that flying increases with wealth, and a 2020 study found that only 4% of the world's population took an international flight in 2018.[26] This is a question of social justice: a tiny share of the world's travellers is responsible for a large share of global warming – just 1% of the world's population accounts for more than half of the emissions from aviation every year. Some super-emitters taking private jets were responsible for emitting up to 7,500 tonnes of CO2 annually; in contrast the average UK emissions per capita per year in 2019 were 5.3 tonnes of CO2.[27] Although Heathrow Airport has long claimed that the main demand for expansion comes from business travellers, even its own figures suggest that before COVID-19 business travel only accounted for 33% of passenger footfall.

Aviation has also enjoyed comfortable taxation. In 1944 world economies came together in Chicago, during the dying days of the Second World War, to agree rules for international aviation. The use of fighter planes had been decisive in the war, and there was a realisation that increasing connections between countries could help the postwar recovery. The Chicago Convention was signed in 1944, and all signatory countries agreed not to impose tax on aviation fuel. This tax-free system persists today, and according to some analyses is the fundamental problem behind rising aviation emissions – no tax on kerosene makes flying uncompetitively cheap compared with other forms of transport using fuels that are taxed. It is a policy which seems out of step with the modern economy; 'removing the constraint of artificially low fuel prices will provide the circumstances to transform the industry'.[28] Without global action it is unlikely that any country would break ranks and begin to tax aviation fuel, and if they did airlines could just move to another jurisdiction. This impact – policies aimed at tackling emissions in one country actually end up causing more emissions in another – is known as carbon leakage. Further, price pressures could lead to what is known as tankering, aircraft refuelling in countries where fuel is cheaper and flying around the world carrying more fuel than they would otherwise need, making them heavier and less efficient.

A few nascent attempts have been made to require aviation to pay its way. The UK was the first country in the world to introduce an aircraft passenger tax, adding a small amount to the average ticket price (£26 to most European destinations). A carbon-pricing signal that applies to international aviation and is having some success is the EU Emissions Trading Scheme (EU ETS), which currently covers flights only within the bloc. The EU ETS is a 'cap-and-trade' scheme: the EU sets a legal limit for emissions over a period of time and grants a fixed number of permits to emit; those limits become progressively stricter over time. The UK formally left the scheme when it withdrew from the EU at the end of 2020.

As signatory countries are obliged to ratchet up their climate ambition following global adoption of the Paris Agreement, there is a growing frustration that aviation has been given *carte blanche* to pollute while other sectors are working hard to decarbonise. That position is becoming increasingly difficult to defend. Although international aviation still makes up a comparatively small proportion of global emissions, as a sector it has the potential to undo all the good work that has been achieved in cutting emissions in other sectors with rapid growth expected in developing countries, particularly China and India. In the UK, the CCC told the government in 2019 that 'a more ambitious target is likely to be required' if IAS emissions were not included in the Net Zero target. In other words, cuts in other sectors such as waste management, agriculture and transport would need to go deeper, possibly even to negative emissions, to accommodate lack of progress on decarbonising aviation. And crucially for this story, the CCC has also said we must have no more net expansion of the UK's airport sector, unless the sector improves its current trajectory. The plans for a third runway at Heathrow Airport seemed to make a mockery of that. According to the new Net Zero target, the carbon budget for the whole of UK aviation is the equivalent of 23 megatonnes of CO2 (23MtCO2e) a year by 2050. The Department for Transport's (DfT) own projections suggest that if the third runway goes ahead, the UK aviation sector would be emitting 40MtCO2e a year by 2050.

Non-CO2 warming

The exception made for aviation does not end there. Flying releases other greenhouse gases which behave in complex ways when they are emitted in the stratosphere and upper troposphere.

Early research into this 'non-CO2 warming' was carried out in the late 1990s. An important report by the IPCC in 1999 called attention to the differences between carbon dioxide and non-carbon dioxide impacts of aviation.[29] The combustion of kerosene emits gases such as nitrogen oxides (collectively, NOx). The gases act in complex ways, changing the way the sun's radiation is absorbed or reflected. They can affect the balance between the amounts of solar energy entering and leaving the Earth's atmosphere. Positive 'radiative forcing' makes the atmosphere hotter and negative makes it cooler. NOx gases are known to interact with the protective ozone layer in the upper troposphere and lower stratosphere; ozone is also a greenhouse gas which contributes to global heating. The IPCC report estimated that by 1992 aircraft emissions had contributed to a 6% increase in global ozone levels, and found that NOx interactions at higher altitudes increase radiative forcing.

Planes also release particles such as soot and water vapour. Water vapour freezes to form high clouds and contrails – the long thin clouds that form in a plane's wake in the upper troposphere. These contrails can also have positive or negative effects on radiative forcing depending on the altitude at which they are emitted.[30] They can then develop into cirrus clouds which can have a similar warming effect by trapping heat.

There has long been scientific debate about the total impact of these non-CO2 emissions. Generally these other gases remain in the atmosphere for less time than carbon dioxide, which can stay there for hundreds of years. Contrails tend to concentrate along flight paths, depend on weather conditions and can dissipate relatively quickly after the plane has passed. These behavioural differences make the gases' contribution to climate change difficult to model. The 1999 report retained some uncertainty about the cumulative impact of these complex chemical reactions and how long they last for. Moreover, they might also contribute to a counter-balancing planetary cooling, which was not well understood.

Nevertheless, the 1999 IPCC report estimated that the increased radiative forcing caused by the high-altitude release of these other emissions was twice to four times that caused by the aircraft's $CO2$ emissions alone.[31] In the intervening twenty years this figure has been revised, but not dramatically. Research in 2020 suggested that the multiple was in the middle of this range: '$CO2$-warming-equivalent emissions based on global warming potentials indicate that aviation emissions are currently warming the climate at approximately three times the rate of that associated with aviation $CO2$ emissions alone'.[32] The DfT's own analysis, which acknowledges the scientific complexities involved in balancing the negative and positive effects of non-$CO2$ emissions and quantifying how long these effects last, nevertheless agrees with the consensus of a positive multiplier of two or three.[33] It is worth noting that, even if NOx gases, water and soot stay in the atmosphere for less time than $CO2$, this does not negate the effect they have while still present.

However, when the ANPS was being drawn up, Secretary of State for Transport Chris Grayling and others argued that there was still considerable uncertainty about the chemical mechanisms behind a number of processes interacting with each other. Whereas the politicians decided that this meant non-$CO2$ warming effects need not be taken into account, Friends of the Earth felt that it meant precisely the opposite. In the Heathrow JR, FoE argued that not knowing the precise impacts of non-$CO2$ radiative forcing does not mean that we should just ignore them. In other words, the ANPS should be drawn up using the important environmental consideration known as the precautionary principle.

This approach is not one which has historically been shared by the UK's regulatory, political and advisory leadership. In 2009, the CCC refrained from recommending any limit be set for non-CO2 emissions because of their 'short-lived effects and uncertainty over how to measure and report their impact in the emissions inventory'.[34] Even in 2020 when the sixth carbon budget was published under CCA 08, the CCC declined to formally recommend that non-CO2 effects be included in emissions reductions targets. As late as 2017 Chris Grayling said that the Aviation Strategy due for publication in 2020 would not include non-CO2 emissions because of this lack of agreement on the scale of their impacts. Nor have non-CO2 aviation emissions been included in the EU ETS, ICAO's CORSIA scheme or the Paris Agreement. This ambivalence was seized upon by Lord Anderson in his submission on behalf of Heathrow Airport at the Supreme Court hearing in October 2020, where he argued that the CCC's lack of recommendation and the lack of scientific and political consensus undermined FoE's argument.

In May 2019, the policy recommendations were beginning to catch up. The CCC's Net Zero pathways report recommended that action on non-CO2 warming should be laid out in the imminent Aviation Strategy. The strategy, which includes the decarbonisation element 'Jet Zero', was finally published in July 2021 after being repeatedly delayed following the coronavirus pandemic. The CCC had recommended that the government should '[m]onitor non-CO2 effects of aviation, set a minimum goal of no further warming [from non-CO2 emissions] after 2050, research mitigation options, and consider how best to tackle non-CO2 effects alongside UK climate targets without increasing CO2 emissions'.[35] However the Jet Zero document goes no further than a commitment to study the problem further, and argues that rolling out new forms of aviation fuel will help to reduce the impact of non-CO2 gases.

Policy peculiarity

> The emissions from aviation are at high altitude, out of sight, out of mind and out of control.[36]

While many people are beginning to question their diet choices, or considering buying an electric car with a view to reducing personal carbon emissions, at least before the coronavirus pandemic hit reducing flying appeared to have fewer advocates. Flying has been viewed as an unquestionably positive thing; take this line from the introduction to the Airports National Policy Statement: 'the positive impacts of the aviation sector extend beyond its direct contribution to the economy by enabling activity in the ... business services, financial services and creative industries'.[37] Airlines and airports are of course designed to encourage ever greater demand for flying, and airlines tend to have tight profit margins. Projections of 70% passenger growth from industry bodies such as Sustainable Aviation UK show that the mood music for airlines is that growth will and must continue. It remains politically difficult to suggest that flying should be constrained, or even that it should be subject to the same decarbonisation and taxation regimes as other industries. As we will see in Chapter 4, the Johnson government seems ideologically set against the idea of any kind of constraint on the growth of air passenger demand. This seems to reflect a belief that no-one wants to be told that they cannot go on a sunshine break or see their family in another country. Along with the technological challenges associated with zero-carbon flight, and the difficulties of where to ascribe responsibility for the emissions from flying, these peculiarities are part of the explanation of why aviation has been left out of key international and domestic laws to tackle climate change.

International attempts to regulate aviation

The only opportunity for a concrete commitment to reduce emissions from flying under the Paris Agreement is in the option for individual countries to include domestic aviation in an NDC. In practice, if all countries did so this would represent about 35% of the total emissions from flying: international emissions make up 65%. This glaring omission is the legacy of a decision by the UNFCCC to not include aviation and shipping in emissions reduction targets when the Kyoto Protocol was drawn up in 1997. Aviation (and shipping) emissions have been historically measured in what are known as international bunker fuels, or fuel that is purchased at airports (or ports) during refuelling. The cross-border nature of aviation and shipping makes it difficult to know which country should be responsible for the emissions from these fuels – the country from which the plane or ship departs, the country at which it arrives or refuels, the country in which the airline or shipowner is based, or based on the nationality/ies of the passenger(s). This conundrum was so intractable that in 1997 bunker fuels were excluded from the Kyoto Protocol for lack of agreement (and perhaps because at that time aviation seemed an insignificant contributor to climate change).

The UNFCCC decided instead that responsibility for making progress on emissions reductions from the two sectors should fall on the specialist UN agencies ICAO and the International Maritime Organisation. As ICAO and the UNFCCC were both established by international treaties, they have the same legal force and almost all nations are members. The UK government has supported the approach of dealing with aviation as an international problem. However, many have argued that ICAO, as an industry body, is better set up to promote aviation than to regulate it. According to the Aviation Environment Federation (AEF) this decision to move responsibility away from Kyoto to the ICAO '... created a policy black hole that has never been properly addressed since'.[38] The ICAO has not yet solved the complexities of attributing responsibility in a convincing way, especially since so many international carriers operate from rich countries. Nearly twenty-five years after Kyoto, passenger miles continue to increase rapidly and since 1987 global emissions from flying have doubled. Aviation now contributes between 2% and 2.5% of total CO_2 emissions.[39]

Despite the difficulties at earlier CoP negotiations, there was early optimism that aviation emissions would be included in the final text of the Paris Agreement when the negotiators arrived in December 2015. References were made to the sector in several early draft texts, with suggested policy measures ranging from emissions reduction targets to a levy on bunker fuels which would be used to contribute towards adaptation funds. References to reducing emissions from bunker fuels survived in the negotiating draft until the last week of CoP21 in Paris, but were removed three days before the final agreement was announced. This 'politics of omission' seemed a response to the particularly problematic debates over aviation, much of which evoked the difficulties surrounding differentiation and the disparity in responsibility for emissions between developed and developing countries. Whereas less developed countries have small or non-existent aviation sectors, many of the old Annex 1 countries were home to multiple carriers. The resulting decision to leave a formal commitment for aviation out of the agreement was a 'missed opportunity'.[40]

The Paris Agreement does provide a number of indirect opportunities to break the *impasse* over aviation emissions. It did put in place an ambitious temperature goal, which requires global emissions to peak soon and then rapidly decline; this is to be achieved by economy-wide reductions implying action will eventually need to be forthcoming from the aviation industry. There is further room for progress in Paris' recognition of the need for urgency and the role non-state actors can play; in this case the aviation industry could be regarded as one. Article 6 mentions the relevance of public and private participation, and the text offers other options for developing market-based measures such as emissions trading.

Global offsetting

ICAO's approach regulating global aviation emissions is known as CORSIA, the Carbon Offsetting and Reduction Scheme for International Aviation. It is a market-based approach which creates credits to offset the 'right to pollute' (these could be certificates for supporting renewable projects or tree-planting, often in other countries), which airlines can trade. Once these permits have all been traded, any rise in emissions from 2020 levels would need to be offset elsewhere in the economy. CORSIA does not aim to reduce emissions from current levels, nor to restrict demand for flights in the future. It merely aims to deploy market measures to ensure that any *growth* in the number of airline passengers or flights from 2020 onwards is theoretically carbon-neutral. Technological and efficiency improvements also sit alongside trading the right to pollute; ICAO currently aims for a 2% improvement in efficiency, year on year. CORSIA forbids double counting: for example, India might sell permits to offset emissions against a reforestation project, or count that project's benefits in its own domestic NDC, but may not do both. There is also an option for airlines to purchase CORSIA-accredited fuels (for example sustainable aviation fuel, SAF, discussed in Chapter 4) which, if properly formulated, should emit less GHGs. Progress in this area might help an airline reduce its obligations to offset.

Monitoring of emissions began in 2019 and the scheme was due to start in 2021. It has already drawn criticism. The AEF argues that it is essentially a political compromise to require the airlines to commit to action without having to curtail the expected enormous growth in aviation demand – at least before the COVID-19 pandemic affected the global airline industry so significantly. CORSIA was particularly criticised because it requires no actual reduction in total emissions from the sector, while every other sector of the global economy is being required to cut emissions quickly. Left unchecked, some estimates predict that aviation emissions could grow to consume a quarter of the global carbon budget by 2050.[41] The mitigation gap that CORSIA needs to cover has been estimated at between 1.6 and 3.7 GtCO2e over its operational period (2021–35), raising questions about how much of the offset capacity available worldwide will be taken up by the needs of the aviation industry.

CORSIA is also silent on how to deal with the non-CO_2 warming impacts of aviation, which we have already seen may be thrice as significant as the CO_2 alone, albeit over a shorter time frame. CORSIA also places no requirement on private jets to mitigate emissions, even though these have a significantly higher carbon footprint per passenger than commercial flights. There is a lack of clarity over exactly what constitutes an effective (and verifiable) offset, with some suggestions that using lower-carbon fuels could still qualify as an offset, a concept which has been criticised.[42] The scheme only operates on a voluntary basis until 2027 and whether it continues or not is due to be reviewed in 2032. Various exemptions, for example for small or less developed countries, suggest that around 20% of potential increases in passenger numbers after 2020 may not be covered by CORSIA.[43]

According to one academic assessment, these limitations would have significant impact on CORSIA's ability to reduce overall CO_2 emissions. The study modelled the system's projected impact in Sweden, and the authors concluded that without additional policy measures to dampen demand, such as the introduction of a passenger air tax, CORSIA could be expected to deliver just a 0.8% reduction in CO_2 emissions. They found that if non-CO_2 emissions are included in the projections, emissions from aviation would actually *increase* under CORSIA. The authors somewhat drolly conclude that '[t]his is much less than what is needed to achieve the 2°C target',[44] a target which in itself is increasingly discredited.

EU Emissions Trading Scheme (EU ETS)

CORSIA can be compared with the more ambitious EU Emissions Trading Scheme, which covers about 40% of the bloc's carbon emissions. From 2012 it also covered flights within the European Union. The scheme requires all airlines operating in Europe, European and non-European alike, to monitor, report and verify emissions. Each receives tradeable allowances covering a certain level of emissions from their flights per year. The allowances are projected to reduce in a linear fashion, ratcheting up ambition, with the last allowance to be issued in 2057. EU ETS does not permit the use of offsetting, and instead has a cap, or set of emissions reductions to 2030. The scheme has seen some success. EU figures suggest that, since 2012, EU ETS has reduced the carbon footprint of the bloc's aviation industry by 17MtCO2e per year.[45]

However, the EU ETS has never reached full implementation. In 2013, just as the EU was about to implement a requirement for airlines to surrender emissions allowances for flights in and out of the Community (i.e. *global* emissions), objections from countries around the world meant that the Union 'stopped the clock'. This move was designed to give time to ICAO to come up with its own scheme, which could be rolled out to all countries and be politically acceptable to other nations. Countries (notably India, China and Brazil) argued that without global action the EU system alone would not reduce emissions from aviation anything like enough. Critics argued that this was further evidence of stalling by airline companies. ICAO then came under pressure from non-EU countries and the airline industry to initiate a global trading scheme, but it took another four years, until 2016, before the scope of

CORSIA was agreed. The EU Council confirmed in June 2020 that EU members would participate in CORSIA. However, there are also concerns from some European countries that because CORSIA is not as stringent as EU ETS, in the longer term the existence of two parallel schemes may undermine the ambition of emissions reduction targets.

Domestic aviation emissions regulation

Aviation was also left out of the UK's CCA 08. As described above, under the Act a series of five-year carbon budgets are applied to every economic sector; but the Act does not formally include IAS, on the basis that it was unclear how to allot international emissions between countries. It did require IAS to be included formally by 2012, unless the government could explain why this was not possible. In that year, the government successfully argued that international aviation emissions were best tackled using an international system, which was at that time EU ETS.

While emissions were not formally included in the UK's domestic targets through sector-specific carbon budgets, CCA 08 requires them to be accounted for using the arcane 'headroom' system. This effectively meant that, for planning purposes, a possible level of aviation emissions was 'assumed' alongside reductions legally mandated for other sectors, under the old 80% reduction target, which aimed to constrain the temperature rise to 2°C. This 'planning assumption' was set at 37.5MtCO2e and when the CCC again advised the government on possible ways to deal with aviation emissions in 2012, the government confirmed that the assumption should be met through EU or global policies (i.e. EU ETS).

Building the UK's climate change framework

Not until the Net Zero decision in 2019 did there seem to be movement towards formally budgeting for IAS emissions in the UK's target. A letter from Lord Deben, the chair of the CCC in September 2019, made the choice stark for the UK's overall decarbonisation trajectory: 'without this [including IAS] a more ambitious target is likely to be required';[46] in other words, other sectors would need to work harder if aviation did not share the burden. In the letter, Lord Deben emphasised that although aviation only made up 7% of UK GHG emissions in 2018, it looked likely to be the sector emitting the most carbon by 2050, even with significant improvements in technology.

THE STORY OF HEATHROW EXPANSION

'I'm not really a natural activist,' Justine Bayley tells me as we take a stroll through Harmondsworth, the village which lies right in the way of the proposed north-west runway. It's a perfect crisp autumn morning, there are two red kites circling in the blue sky above and a middle-aged couple out for a country cycle are basking in the sun on the village green. Justine is tired; 'I just want to be left alone to enjoy my life and my house without the worry of this airport expansion every day,' she says.

Justine's old house is covered in a rampant wisteria plant, and her front garden is home to two dwarf apple trees. Her garden opens out onto the well-kept village green; opposite is the Gable village stores and the Crown pub. It's a very traditional English scene.

'The perimeter fence for the runway would be right there,' she says, pointing to the back gardens of some 1930s houses about 150m from her front door. 'That whole area of housing will be gone, the road will be sliced in two, the back of the pub will be the boundary. Can you imagine having planes landing and taking off that close to your house every single day?'

A drive around Harmondsworth and Sipson with Justine, and it's easy to see how there is very little land left into which Heathrow Airport could expand. During the ten-minute drive from West Drayton station, we cross a huge gyratory on the M4, and a bridge over the M4 trunk road to the airport. Harmondsworth and Sipson are already squeezed on all four sides. I can hear a constant hum from the M25 to the west as we walk around; the M4 to the east and the A4 to the north. It is hard to imagine how the arrival of an extra 700 planes a day would not result in an increase in traffic to the area, not to mention the disruption during the construction phase of rerouting the M25 under the new runway.

Justine is the chair of the campaign group Stop Heathrow Expansion (SHE), the face of the local residents' objections to the third runway since the coalition government revived the plans in 2012; SHE is the successor group to the No Third Runway Action Group (NoTrag) which fought expansion in the 2010s, and is a key member of the No Third Runway Coalition, an umbrella group founded in 2017. SHE joined Friends of the Earth and Plan B in support in the court room at the Heathrow JR hearing, although they did not take part in the case. 'Bringing in the climate case has been really important,' she says, 'It's an issue that has been swept under the carpet for a long time. We still have our local campaign focusing on traffic, pollution and noise, but it feels like it's going to be decided on these national issues now.'

Justine takes me on a walk to visit the pretty, eleventh-century St Mary's church, hidden behind yew trees and a flint-stone wall. A few metres further and we walk through a creaking gate to see the Harmondsworth Great Tithe Barn. The Grade 1-listed building is described by English Heritage as ranking 'alongside the Houses of Parliament and Westminster Abbey for its exceptional architectural and historic interest'. It's an enormous building, originally used for storing crops before threshing; it's some 60m long and held up by thirteen oak tresses. Three or four aeroplanes come in to land as we talk, causing us to pause briefly. Justine shows me a picture of a little owl that was spotted flying inside the barn by local schoolchildren. The barn has remained intact since the fifteenth century, but for a time was threatened with demolition by the earlier Heathrow expansion plans. After the community campaigned to protect the barn, the plans were amended. The boundary of the proposed development was moved, but only about 200m away.

Like many journalists before me who have been out to visit the north Heathrow villages, I'm surprised at how pretty Harmondsworth is. There is clearly a sense of community here. It's an old place with a proud sense of history. Further down the road at Sipson (and another village, Longford, which would be almost completely lost under the tarmac), there is a more transient feel. Justine tells me that Heathrow Airport bought up many of the properties in Sipson in anticipation of the previous attempt at expansion, and now these are rented out on a short-term basis. In Longford, along with some residential estates there is some temporary accommodation for asylum seekers and a couple of airport hotels.

The airport expansion is clearly a divisive issue in all the villages and not everyone is fuming at the plans. Some residents are content with an offer of 25% above market rate for the 700-odd properties covered by the compulsory purchase property scheme, and look forward to starting a new life elsewhere.[1] Some have just had enough. Others work at the airport and want to see its fortunes restored after the coronavirus pandemic, along with the prospect of new jobs and opportunities.

Many of those who are opposed to the plans have lived in the area a long time, and the real problem for them is exhaustion – for more than twenty years there has been no respite from uncertainty. Many celebrated the abandoning of the runway expansion announced by then prime minister David Cameron in 2010, only to find their lives turned upside down again just two years later. Some campaigners are in their 80s and have decided enough is enough. Lots of homes are not covered by compulsory purchase but still have been offered a price 25% above market if they do decide to move further down the line. What will the market price look like with one of the world's biggest airports quite literally on the doorstep? Who wants to send their children to a school which may be demolished? Does Harmondsworth still have a future?

Back in Justine's kitchen, we watch the birds in her back garden. 'I feel like I've been in suspended animation for more than twenty years,' says Justine over coffee and home-baked biscuits. 'I've been on the edge of my seat all that time and I really don't know how much longer I can stand it'.

A third runway at Heathrow Airport has been mooted since the late 1990s. Campaigners like Justine have fought several attempts at expansion over that period. The airport today is one of the busiest in the world, a long way from its humble beginnings. It started life as the Great West Aerodrome on land near the hamlet of Heath Row in 1930. The site was requisitioned during the Second World War, when it became RAF Heston for a brief period, a base for troop-carrying aircraft bound for the far east. On 1 January 1946 the site was handed over to the Air Ministry to become London's new civil airport. By 1951 the airport had handled almost 800,000 passengers. By the time Heathrow celebrated its 60th anniversary in 2006 it had handled around 1.4bn passengers on over 14m flights, and boasted four terminals with a fifth in construction.[2]

Despite this huge growth, the airport has long been dogged by capacity issues. Before the coronavirus pandemic hit, Heathrow was regularly running at 98% capacity, with many planes having to circle the skies over London in holding patterns, waiting for a slot to land. Airport bosses have argued since the late 1990s that a third runway would help to ease congestion, which was costing businesses and delaying passengers. However, the airport's location to the west of London does not make this easy to achieve without major disruption. First of all, there is the problem of large numbers of aircraft flying over residential areas. Pilots prefer to land aircraft into the wind, because the plane has a slower ground speed at touchdown which in turn reduces the length of runway needed. The prevailing wind in London is westerly which means that, around 70% of the time,[3] aeroplanes have to approach Heathrow from the east – flying over swathes of south-east, south-west and west London as they descend. This means that on busy days large parts of London see a steady stream of planes coming in to land at intervals of not much more than ninety seconds or so. There is also the difficulty of squeezing another runway in among the developments already there. A cursory look at the map of Heathrow shows it is almost encircled; to the east and north are residential areas and the M4 motorway, to the north the A4, and to the west the M25. Heathrow is also situated in green belt land which means extra restrictions apply to development in that area.

Heathrow is the UK's main hub airport and the UK's busiest. The hub model means that it serves a large number of passengers coming in to change planes and travel on to other destinations. The hub model is a way of pooling demand for destinations and regular flights. Routes are made more viable and profitable by filling more flights with passengers using Heathrow as a transit point. Heathrow has direct connections with 9 regional airports in the UK, and serves 180 destinations in 85 countries. More than half of the passengers passing through Heathrow every year are on long-haul flights. Smaller airports such as Gatwick and Luton are known as 'point-to-point': most flights from them are direct to short-haul destinations.

Heathrow Airport was privatised in 1987 when the old British Airports Authority became BAA plc. In 2006 BAA plc was bought by a consortium led by Spanish firm Ferrovial, and in 2009 the company was forced to sell its other UK airports (Gatwick, Stansted and others) under competition laws. Renamed Heathrow Airport Holdings Limited (from now on referred to as Heathrow Airport), the airport makes much of its money from landing charges on incoming flights and services it offers to passengers and airlines. Since the early 1990s, Heathrow has been signalling that it needs more capacity to allow it to compete with other major European hub airports, and increasingly Middle Eastern hubs such as Dubai and Istanbul which have grown enormously this century. In Europe, the main competitors are Amsterdam Schiphol, Paris Charles de Gaulle (which Air France-KLM uses as a hub) and Frankfurt (Lufthansa). In 2019, Frankfurt provided the best hub connectivity in the world,[4] offering more than twice as many connections as Heathrow. Amsterdam Schiphol Airport in the Netherlands has twenty links with UK regional airports,[5] more than twice as many as Heathrow. Heathrow was still the busiest airport in Europe on total passenger numbers until it was overtaken by Charles de Gaulle in 2020,[6] but while other European destinations still have scope for expansion, Heathrow has little or none. Heathrow is hobbled by only having two runways, one for take-off and one for landing. In comparison, Charles de Gaulle has four runways and Schiphol has six.

For many years Heathrow Airport has joined with business leaders and unions to argue that without expansion the UK will miss out on opportunities to expand its global connectivity and economic growth. John Holland-Kaye, Heathrow's CEO, has argued that aviation is the 'cornerstone' of the UK economy, a vital component of the new Global Britain in the realignments taking place following the exit from the European Union. Domestic politics has consistently been on the side of aviation, promoting it as a vital cog in the economy which facilitates trade and personal freedom. However, building a third runway at Heathrow has proved maddeningly elusive. There have been vociferous campaigns on both sides of the debate right from when the idea was first mooted in the late 1990s.

The Terminal Gang

An early taste of the bitter fights to come was the battle to get proposals passed to build a fifth terminal at Heathrow, which would allow 30m more passengers a year to pass through the airport. As passenger numbers soared in the 1970s and 1980s it became evident that the ageing Terminals 1, 2 and 3 would soon be unable to cope, despite Terminal 4 opening in 1986. BAA plc submitted a formal planning application for the construction of a new terminal in 1993. It was a project on an unprecedented scale. The plans involved constructing the largest free-standing building in the UK, 396m long and 40m high. Two rivers had to be diverted, a new railway station constructed and a link road from the M25, and more than a square kilometre of concrete laid for taxiways and aircraft stands. The total cost for the project was to run to £4.3bn.

Nic Ferriday is an unassuming west Londoner. The creases on his face hold the echoes of much laughter, but his gait suggests a tired story of clashing repeatedly against the realities of endless growth at Heathrow. After taking early retirement from British Telecom in the 1990s Nic, who has a degree in physics, found his life being taken over by the plans for Terminal 5. His house in Ealing is affected by noise from the airport, and he was alarmed at the prospect of an increase in flights and road congestion as more people travelled to the airport.

Nic joined his local Friends of the Earth group in west London, which had decided to campaign against the construction of Terminal 5. Friends of the Earth has a central office coordinating activities in England, Wales and Northern Ireland across a large network of autonomous local groups which can request support from the centre but essentially choose their own campaigning activities. FoE groups in west London wanted to campaign against the construction of Terminal 5 on the grounds of increased noise pollution, increased air pollution particularly from the expected additional road traffic, and the loss of green space and habitats.

There were also fears among the campaigners that the new terminal would be a Trojan horse to ease the way to approval for a third runway. At that time, in the early 1990s, BAA had never openly called for a new runway. In fact, Heathrow

CEO Sir John Egan had written to local residents during the Terminal 5 inquiry to assure them that the company was not planning to ask for one. But the campaigners did not trust the airport. Aviation was growing fast with the emergence of low-cost carriers Ryanair and easyJet in the late 1990s. The Labour party had made no secret of its desire to improve accessibility to flying for greater numbers of people. The capacity issues at Heathrow were only going to get worse.

The Planning Inquiry into Terminal 5 at Heathrow, headed by Ray Vandemeer QC, ended up becoming the UK's longest inquiry ever. Nic Ferriday attended about a day-and-a-half a week for almost four-and-a-half years. When it finally concluded in March 1999, the inquiry had clocked up 525 sitting days and £80m in costs; 800 witnesses had given evidence, 21 million words been spoken and 80,000 separate documents generated. Nearly 23,000 people made written submissions, 95% of which opposed the plans. A group of lawyers representing all sides became known as the 'Terminal Gang', staking out a conference room built over a boarded-up swimming pool at the Ramada Hotel in Heathrow's hinterlands. At the hotel twenty-six rooms were converted to offices for the inquiry, filled with documents and computers.

Not surprisingly, the inquiry was criticised as having been a monumental waste of time. Its defenders argued that it was a chance for people to have their say, its detractors felt that, despite its extraordinary length, the decision had been made before it sat. In November 2001 the Secretary of State for Transport, Local Government and the Regions, Stephen Byers, announced his decision. Terminal 5 was given the go-ahead, but with conditions. Due to the overwhelming concerns over noise impacts, the number of flights was to be capped at 480,000 per year, there would be no increase in the geographical area within which noise could exceed a threshold (57 decibels – World Health Organization guidelines state that 'annoyance' will occur between 50 and 55DB) and a further consultation was to be held to review the rules for night flights. Crucially, the planning inspector recommended that a third runway would have 'unacceptable environmental consequences' and advised against it; somewhat oddly, as this question was not formally laid before the inquiry. Stephen Byers was less clear, saying it was not necessary at that stage to reach a conclusion on whether a new runway might be needed, or where it might be located. Instead, he committed the Labour government to further consideration, involving drawing up a White Paper on further airport expansion, particularly in London and the south-east. Friends of the Earth hit back, arguing that it was inconsistent to agree to cap flights while simultaneously arguing that a plan for further expansion would be needed. With this one mention of a third runway, the stage had been set for a monumental battle over Heathrow expansion plans for years to come.

The fall-out from the Terminal 5 Planning Inquiry would eventually provide some impetus for the passing of the Planning Act in 2008, which aimed to speed up and streamline planning applications. The Act would form the basis of the legal challenge against the Heathrow expansion plans more than twenty years after the inquiry.

The first battle of Heathrow expansion

By 2003, the Labour government's view was clear. In December, following a public consultation with some half a million responses, the long-awaited Aviation White Paper written by the Department for Transport was launched, containing ambitious plans for airport expansion. The paper set out a strategic framework within which authorities and the aviation industry could plan expansion, and gave guidance on how future planning applications might be decided. This would allow private companies (airport owners and operators) to bring forward specific proposals for expansion. The paper anticipated a trebling of passengers in UK airports by 2030, and there in black and white were proposals for new runways at Heathrow and Stansted. Of further concern to campaigners in west London, changes to the practice of runway alternation at Heathrow were also proposed. This involves planes landing over west London switching runways at 3pm to give communities living below some respite. Consideration had been given to other schemes in the south-east, but due to an agreement signed in 1979, the option of building a second runway at Gatwick was put on ice, and plans for a Thames Estuary airport, possibly at Cliffe, were rejected on cost and practicability grounds. It was thought that Luton still had enough capacity to allow for expansion without another runway. The paper also mooted new runways in other parts of the country – in Scotland and possibly Birmingham – longer runways at Newcastle, Bristol and Leeds Bradford, and terminal development at Manchester.

While the White Paper clearly noted that communities living close to airport infrastructure were concerned about air quality and noise, and recognised the growing contribution of aviation to global climate change, the economic argument clearly dominated. The first words of the report, a foreword from Alistair Darling, Secretary of State for Transport, set the tone: 'Air travel is essential to the United Kingdom's economy and to our continued prosperity'.[7] The paper acknowledged the problem of rising GHG emissions from aviation, and stated a commitment to dealing with that at the international level. Mitigation of emissions was to be achieved through emissions trading schemes.

The White Paper ignited a fierce campaign of resistance in west London communities. In 2000, a coalition of groups concerned about disturbance from Heathrow and the possibility of further expansion had come together under the umbrella group Airport Watch. Campaign groups such as HACAN ClearSkies (Heathrow Association for the Control of Aircraft Noise) and NoTRAG (No Third Runway Action Group), which campaigned for local people in Harmondsworth and Sipson whose communities faced destruction if the plans for a third runway went ahead, were joined by some of the country's biggest environmental campaign groups, such as FoE, Greenpeace, the World Wide Fund for Nature (WWF), the Campaign to Protect Rural England (CPRE) and the Royal Society for the Protection of Birds (RSPB), and cross-party representatives from local and national government. MPs such as Justine Greening (Conservative), Susan Kramer (Liberal Democrats) and Kate Hoey and John McDonnell (Labour) represented constituencies under the flight path affected by noise and disturbance. The London mayor (then Ken Livingstone) joined local authorities Wandsworth, Richmond, Hillingdon and Hounslow to openly oppose expansion. In 2007, Plane Stupid joined the coalition. This group advocated non-violent direct action in order to raise awareness of climate change and took part in a series of climate camps including one just outside Sipson, near Heathrow's boundary. Plane Stupid hit the headlines with other high-profile stunts including invading an aviation conference in London, and one in which activist Dan Glass superglued himself to the new prime minister Gordon Brown's sleeve during a Downing Street reception to recognise his campaign work.

In November 2007, the new Secretary of State for Transport, Ruth Kelly, launched the 'Adding capacity at Heathrow Airport' consultation in November 2007. The consultation involved plans for a third 2,200m runway and a sixth terminal, north of the A4. Three conditions were set – a limit on the size of the 'contour' (geographical area) within which noise levels could exceed 57 decibels, adherence to the EU limit on NO_2 (nitrogen dioxide) levels of 40 μg/m^3 and better access to the new terminal by public transport. Kelly also published a report detailing how the government wanted to push for aviation's GHG emissions to be included in the EU ETS, then a fledgling scheme (see Chapter 1 for details).

Airport Watch was ready. 'We had no intention of using this consultation in the traditional way,' said John Stewart, the chair of HACAN for over twenty years until he stepped down in 2020. While just a handful of information events were organised by the DfT, the coalition went all out to oppose the plans. The group held around forty meetings, to which they estimated 20,000 people turned up. Key figures such as Caroline Lucas and the Liberal Democrats' Sarah Ludford spoke. Greenpeace activists climbed onto a plane at Heathrow and the coalition launched its own economic analysis of the expansion project. Airport Watch organised a rally at Westminster Central Hall which attracted around 2,500 people, and twelve years to the day before the Court of Appeal judgment would blow a hole in the reincarnated version of the Heathrow expansion plans, Plane Stupid managed to climb onto the roof of the Houses of Parliament and unveil a giant banner with the words 'BAA Headquarters'. The activist group made paper aeroplanes out of emails between the DfT and Heathrow that they'd printed out, which had offered advice on where to move air pollution monitors so they would not record illegal levels of pollution.

In the end party politics tipped the balance. Several prominent Conservative MPs including Justine Greening, John Randall and Theresa May consistently spoke out about the impact of expansion on their constituencies, at a time when leader of the Opposition David Cameron was laying out a vision of a caring conservatism prioritising environmental action. Theresa Villiers, the party's transport spokesperson, began to intimate that, if elected, the Conservatives would oppose expansion. The stance was confirmed at the party conference in autumn 2008, where Villiers announced that the Conservatives would advocate a high-speed rail link instead (later to become HS2). But Labour ploughed on. In January 2009, new transport secretary Geoff Hoon announced the government's decision. It was a surprise to few – the third runway was given the go-ahead, with three strict conditions on noise, public transport and air pollution attached. However, by this point Gordon Brown's premiership was becoming deeply unpopular and many were openly talking about the prospect of Labour losing the election due in 2010. The tide appeared to be turning against the expansion plans. David Cameron, the man being widely tipped as the next prime minister, visited Richmond in September 2009 where he famously declared 'no ifs, no buts, there'll be no third runway at Heathrow'.

The campaign against the third runway secured a significant victory just two months before the election, with a judicial review case which used very similar arguments to those which would be run again ten years later. In March 2010, a coalition of groups including WWF, Greenpeace, CPRE, John Stewart and HACAN and a number of local MPs, argued in the High

Court that the climate impacts of the proposed third runway had not been taken seriously enough. The campaigners argued that the Aviation White Paper from 2003, the document which first suggested official support for a third runway, was hopelessly out of date. They argued that the considerable developments in climate policy in the intervening years and the understanding of the impact of aviation on the UK's total emissions meant that the expansion plans should not go ahead. In a complex judgment, Lord Justice Carnwath sent the government's planning proposal back to the DfT for further consideration. He said that the government's public consultation did not take account of the latest information on economic benefits and the costs of climate change and was based on figures which were eight years old.[8] While not completely ruling out the development, Lord Carnwath hinted at the battles to come by stating that the proposed new ANPS would need to take into account the more up-to-date landscape of climate change policy.

In the end the legal arguments were subsumed in the political upheaval of May 2010. The general election took the country into uncharted territory. Both Labour and the Conservatives failed to win a majority, and eventually the Liberal Democrats agreed to form a coalition with the Conservatives. The Lib Dems had made no secret of their opposition to the expansion of Heathrow. The new prime minister David Cameron did not disappoint, and a day after the new government was formed it was announced that the third runway plan would be scrapped. Instead, the coalition would pursue the embryonic plans for a new high-speed rail connection to Birmingham and the north (HS2), with a possible connection to Heathrow, which had been mooted by the previous government. The coalition also stated that there would be no new runways at Stansted or

Gatwick Airports. The campaigners were jubilant. 'Never in UK history had the aviation industry suffered such a rebuff,'[9] said HACAN's John Stewart, presumably convinced that the battle over the third runway was over.

The third runway rears its head ... again

But like so many times in this story the excitement was short-lived. By 2012, the third runway was back on the cards. After staking his reputation on opposing it, Cameron appears to have been swayed by lobbying from the industry and back-bench MPs. He approved a new review of the options led by then Chancellor of the Exchequer George Osborne in order to set out 'government thinking on new runways and terminals'. That '... thinking is that he and Cameron are preparing to break their word,' wrote columnist Simon Jenkins. 'West Londoners should feel very afraid.'[10]

Justine Greening's history as a prominent campaigner against airport expansion made her position in the coalition government difficult. She was replaced as transport secretary in September 2012, by Patrick McLoughlin. In September 2012, just days after Greening left, prime minister Cameron announced the establishment of a new Airports Commission. It was to be chaired by Sir Howard Davies, an economist and former head of the Financial Services Authority, with four other commissioners and a support secretariat drawn mostly from the DfT. On taking up his role at the Commission, Davies resigned his position on the International Advisory Board to the Government of Singapore Investment Corporation Private (GIC), which had become one of the owners of Heathrow when BAA plc had been taken over by Ferrovial in 2006 (GIC today owns 11% of the company). The Commission was asked to produce recommendations for improving the use of existing capacity across the UK as a whole, as well as the 'nature, scale and timing of the steps necessary to maintain the UK's status as an international hub for aviation'.[11] Its interim report was due by December 2013, and its final report by summer 2015.

The interim report of December 2013 contained few surprises for the opposition campaigners; more capacity was needed and it would be needed in the south-east. The report argued that there was little scope for persuading customers and airlines to use regional airports to take pressure off London, concluding that there was a 'clear case for one net additional runway in London and the south-east to come into operation by 2020'. The Commission had analysed a number of proposals to tackle the problem, and three options were chosen to be taken forward for further consideration. The first was a new 3,500m runway south of the existing runway at Gatwick, built at a safe distance from the existing tarmac and with a new taxiway and terminal facilities. The second option, described as an innovative solution, had been put forward by a consortium known as Heathrow Hub and led by Jock Lowe, a former Concorde pilot. This option involved lengthening the existing northern runway at Heathrow to 6,000m to allow it to operate essentially as two separate runways. Proponents of this plan argued it would be less expensive and disruptive to build, would require fewer demolitions and compulsory purchases, and would provide carbon savings because aircraft on the tarmac would not have to taxi so far. The third proposal was an entirely new 3,500m runway north-west of the existing airport, which became known as the 'north-west' runway option. This would involve significant development of land to the north of the existing site, to allow for the construction (among other things) of a new terminal building. About 700 homes would need to be demolished and significant new road infrastructure constructed.

The next steps for the Airports Commission would include an assessment of environmental, social and economic impacts, and risks and opportunities associated with each proposal. This would involve testing the commercial and operational viability of all the schemes, and their economic benefits and costs, and working out which scheme fit the 'assessment of need' criteria best (i.e. catered best for an expected growth in demand). At this preliminary stage, expansion at Gatwick appeared to be the least expensive option, with estimates coming in at between £10–13bn. This compared with an estimated £13bn for the extended runway proposal and £17bn for the proposed north-west runway. It also appeared that the Gatwick scheme would have less impact on the local environment, and that it would subject only 6,000 more people to extra noise, while Heathrow schemes might affect 150,000 more people.

The Commission's final report was published on 1 July 2015. After 18 months of deliberations and 70,000 responses to the consultation, the Commission decided that the north-west runway at Heathrow Airport presented the strongest case. This would require a package of measures to address its environmental and community impacts. The report explained that the north-west option was chosen largely because it would have 'more substantial strategic and economic benefits'. The report argued that it would also offer more scope for reducing noise nuisance and have a greater impact on regional economies, which might tap into increased connectivity through new routes opening for domestic flights or freight capacity. The Commission concluded that the north-west scheme was a more reliable proposition than the extended northern runway proposal which involved 'untested infrastructure' and which would not offer the same increase to capacity. Gatwick, although a strong contender, was turned down because the Commission assessed that it would not be able to offer the same rapid increase in the number of long-haul destinations as Heathrow.

The final report of the Airports Commission referenced the CCC's position that 'any change to [the] UK's aviation capacity would have to take place in the context of global climate change, and the UK's policy obligations in this area'. The report integrated the CCC's planning assumptions for the sector into its modelling to see how those would affect projected demand. At that point the planning assumption for aviation – a maximum of 37.5MtCO2e per year by 2050 – had been prepared under the CCA 08 target (an 80% reduction in emissions by 2050, to keep global temperature rises within 2°C above pre-industrial levels). The Airports Commission modelling was based on the assumption that the regulatory framework in the UK (including the UK's participation in market-based measures such as the EU ETS) would keep emissions from aviation within the CCC's planning assumption, and therefore did not try to assess the costs of doing this.

The Airports Commission developed two different sets of forecasts for future aviation demand to decide which of the schemes would most increase capacity. The two models used were 'carbon-capped' and 'carbon-traded'. The carbon-capped scenario assumed that emissions from aviation would not be allowed to grow above the 37.5MtCO2e planning assumption. This scenario allowed no trading of emissions or purchase of offsets and any growth in emissions from aviation would need to be balanced by a reduction in emissions in another sector, the 'waterbed effect'. The carbon-traded model assumed the use of international trading mechanisms such as the EU ETS; the market would ensure that emissions reductions were achieved where it was 'most desirable and cost-effective' to do so.

The measures to mitigate the impact of the north-west runway scheme were ambitious, but mostly focused on noise, traffic and air pollution. The Commission suggested the developers cultivate a new relationship with local communities. Much of this involved tackling the infernal problem of aircraft noise; recommendations included a ban on flights between 11.30pm and 6am, which would be possible now that more landing slots would be available during the day. The Commission also suggested more predictable respite periods and a new, independent, aviation noise authority be established. Their final report also recommended a generous compensation package for those whose homes would be lost, incentives to encourage those working at or travelling to the airport to use public transport and a guarantee that the EU limits for nitrogen dioxide levels around the airport would not be breached by the expansion plans.

'Taken together, these recommendations ensure that an expanded Heathrow can be a better neighbour for local communities than the airport is today, while delivering significantly enhanced connectivity and substantial long-term economic and strategic benefits for the UK as a whole',[12] the Airports Commission's final report concluded. The primacy of aviation in securing the UK's global position was confirmed: 'it is central to ensuring increased productivity, growth and employment opportunities'.

The masterplan – the north-west runway

The plans for a new north-west runway at Heathrow were certainly on a colossal scale. It was the most expensive scheme of the three choices offered to the Airports Commission. The Commission estimated that it would cost around £17.6bn in capital expenditure to complete, largely due to the amount of land it would be necessary to acquire and the huge number of access options required, such as approach roads and rail lines. The Commission estimated that Heathrow Airport would need to raise additional equity of up to £8.4bn and debt of up to £29.9bn, making the investment similar in scale to the National Grid.

The proposed third runway was expected to facilitate an extra 260,000 flights per year (an extra 700 per day), bringing the total to 740,000, comfortably meeting the Commission's 'assessment of need to 2030' for increased capacity. Passenger numbers would reach 132–149m by 2050 (up from 74m in 2015), which would make the airport comparable in size to the new mega-airport being constructed in Istanbul. The Commission's forecasts suggested this could equate to 7–21m more seats on long-haul flights and 15–30m more short-haul seats. By comparison, the Gatwick proposal would facilitate an extra 560,000 flights a year (twice the current number from Gatwick), and the Heathrow Hub plans 700,000 flights per year. The Commission found that the north-west runway option offered the best mix between long-haul and short-haul expansion. It estimated that the scheme would help to create up to 108,000 new jobs by 2050.

The engineering requirements were also enormous. A sixth terminal with capacity for 35m passengers per annum – on a scale similar to Terminal 5 – would be added to the west of the original site. A waste-to-energy plant would need to be moved, requiring its own planning process. The site would also include land set aside for ancillary services, extra commercial development and a number of hotels. Three new car parks would be built with space for 52,000 extra cars, and local rivers would need to be diverted and new drainage areas created. In total the plans required the loss of approximately 900ha of land, 430ha of which is within the green belt.[13] The new surface access options would include rail links (among them, Crossrail and possibly even a link with HS2 at Old Oak Common); significant road upgrading with a diversion of the A4, widening of the M4 and (perhaps the most disruptive of all) rerouting part of the M25 motorway through a tunnel to be dug under the new runway.

The Commission estimated that the number of people affected by noise from overflying would rise under any of the scenarios, but that there was some variation according to which forecast was used. It argued that the third runway would allow a more flexible approach to take-off and landing. With an extra runway, modelling suggested that one runway could be assigned for take-offs, one for landing and the third might alternate between them. The Commission concluded that this would allow greater respite for communities around the airport, especially if runway assignments were regularly changed. In turn the new capacity would mean fewer night flights because more planes would be accommodated during the day. However, a decision on how flight paths could cater for the extra 240,000 flights a year would not be taken until after another consultation. Using a selection of the publicly available indicative flight path maps, an investigation by Greenpeace estimated that up to 1.6m people would be affected by aircraft noise, more than twice the number that had previously been exposed to overflying.[14] On air pollution, the Commission conceded that 'there is clearly a substantial negative impact of the scheme on air quality, unless forceful mitigation measures are implemented'. No immediate solution was forthcoming, but it assured readers that 'further work on this issue is ongoing'.

The case for a third runway

For Heathrow Airport, the case for expansion is clear cut. Without it, the Airport's capacity problems will continue to constrain growth and negatively impact passengers and business. Presumably FGP Topco, the company which owns Heathrow Airport Holdings Limited, also wants to increase its profits by increasing passenger numbers and garnering landing charges from more flights. But Heathrow Airport also has a symbolic value. Much of the media narrative on airport expansion supports the role the airport can play in securing the UK's leading place in a globalised world. Long before the Brexit vote led to the resurgence of the international trade agenda, the Airports Commission noted that both Heathrow and UK plc might lose competitiveness if international competitors (European but also increasingly in the Middle East – Dubai, Istanbul, etc.) were able to grow without planning constraints similar to those seen in the UK. 'Expanding Heathrow will keep Britain as one of the world's great trading nations, right at the heart of the global economy,' said John Hollande-Kaye when the Commission's final report was published in 2015. Many businesses and trade unions spoke out about the importance of job creation, better connections and fewer delays for passengers, all of which were affected by the constraint of only having two runways. It was assumed that demand for more frequent departures and more destinations, particularly among leisure travellers, would only increase.

But of course, any decision about the necessity to expand and the best place to do it would always come down to money. From this point of view it is hard to describe the case for the north-west runway as compelling.

In the final Airports Commission report, the cost–benefit analysis was assessed using a version of the Treasury's standard 'web-tag' analysis for transport projects. This analysis groups the economic benefits of the north-west runway into a number of areas – the economic benefit for passengers, measured by more convenient flight choices, cheaper tickets and reduced delays, the 'consumer surplus'; the 'producer surplus', measured through businesses using the airport, increased trade in goods and services, increased tax revenues and new jobs to be generated locally by 2050. The capital expenditure costs of the scheme, plus the costs of mitigating the negative impacts of expansion (the 'carbon value' per tonne of CO_2), dealing with noise and air pollution problems and compensation packages – were then subtracted. When all of this had been taken into consideration, the Airports Commission examined the possible benefits under the carbon-traded and carbon-capped scenarios. The AC estimated that capital expenditure on the north-west runway project would be £17.6bn. In the carbon-traded scenario, the modelling assessed the net present value (NPV) at a benefit of £11.8bn over sixty years. In the carbon-capped scenario, the NPV was assessed at just £1.4bn, significantly less than the Gatwick proposal (assessed at £5.5bn NPV under the same scenario).

The economic calculations were complex. According to the draft AC, it was expected that at least some of the costs of the improved surface access – roads, rail lines, etc. – would be funded by the government. Heathrow Airport – a private, foreign-owned consortium – would be expected to contribute to the costs of the changes to the M25, which were integral to the scheme. The capital costs of expansion would be expected to be met by the developer, and it looked as though the assessment envisaged at least some of that outlay being recouped through an expected increase in landing charges, which would probably be passed on to customers through ticket prices. Heathrow's landing charges were already some of the highest in Europe – around £22 per passenger in 2019. In 2017, it emerged that the airport had indeed written to the Civil Aviation Authority (CAA: regulator) asking it to agree to the company passing any costs from unexpected problems in construction of the third runway on to passengers and airlines.[15] The question how such costs would be met was raised again during the coronavirus pandemic, which had repeatedly disturbed air travel. The CAA ruled in December 2021 that the airport could increase its charges to over £30 per passenger – up to twice the costs of landing charges at rival airports Paris, Amsterdam and Madrid. This was less than what Heathrow Airport had wanted, but was seen as a portent for how the costs of expansion might be passed on to customers in future.

Because of the unique difficulties of accounting for such a huge international project, two of the experts employed by the Airports Commission said that 'building the economic case is conceptually demanding and has not proved to be straightforward'.[16] The experts argued that sticking to the Treasury Green Book 'web-tag' analysis methodology had been problematic.[17]

In the end a second economic modelling approach was used, known as strategic computable general equilibrium (S-CGE), which even the Airports Commission described as 'novel'.

The results of the S-CGE modelling made it into newspaper headlines when the final report of the Commission was released. In the executive summary of the final report, there was no mention of the results of the standard web-tag analysis, the carbon-capped scenario of which had yielded the rather paltry £1.4bn benefit over sixty years. Instead, a much more sexy £147bn in economic benefits was claimed, resulting from the S-CGE analysis. This figure made it into the executive summary and the strategic assessment of the project. The £1.4bn figure only appeared in a table in the text for the economic analysis section of the final report, and was barely picked up by journalists.

The use of this much higher figure for assessed economic benefits was the subject of controversy. The rival bid team from Gatwick commissioned a report by accounting firm Deloitte – the analysis for the Commission had been carried out by rival firm Price Waterhouse Coopers. S-CGE was described as 'innovative' compared to the well-understood and trusted web-tag transport analysis models. Deloitte's report pointed to concerns that the new method had 'double counted' some of the benefits. It suggested that links between passenger numbers and increased productivity, particularly when the mix between international and national passengers was unclear, should be treated with caution.[18] The analysis showed that little of the projected economic benefit would stem from any international transfer passengers spending actually *in the UK*, because they would never leave the terminal building. Even the DfT's analysis suggested that up to 75% of passengers using the newly expanded hub by 2040 would be international transfer passengers. In fact, much of the economic analysis based on the S-CGE approach was removed from the economic analysis sections of the Airports Commission report by the Department for Transport before the final draft was published, and moved to the strategic case section.

There appeared to be other problems with the modelling of the economic case. When the DfT transcribed the Commission's recommendations into its own documents, it adjusted parts of the report dealing with the climate impacts of the runway. Expert evidence had suggested the potential contribution of carbon trading to reducing emissions had been optimistic. The Commission itself had admitted that 'incorporating the carbon-capped forecasts into an economic assessment presented a number of technical challenges'. It had not fully assessed the costs of 'abating' the emissions from international flights even though this would clearly be necessary to understand the costs required to stay within the CCC's planning assumption. In a substantial critique of the Airports Commission's work published at the time, the AEF and Airport Watch asked why the final report did not include a revised economic appraisal in which the 'carbon values' used in modelling were pushed as high as would be necessary to limit demand enough to keep aviation emissions within the 37.5Mt limit. This was something that the CCC had recommended, but the Airports Commission never did. Nic Ferriday argued that this was because the authors of the Airports Commission report knew that the carbon cost of achieving this would 'dominate' the assessment.

So, it was no secret that the final Airports Commission report found that, of the three schemes examined, the north-west runway would clearly lead to the greatest increase in carbon emissions overall. In contrast Gatwick with its short-haul flight network would have generated the lowest increase. At the same time, some of the analysis behind the economic case was exposed as flawed and the costs of mitigating those carbon impacts were not completely modelled. Even the DfT figures suggested that, in one of the many scenarios they ran, over sixty years a third runway at Heathrow might generate little or no economic benefit or even be a net drain on the UK economy. But even though these flaws in the analysis were pointed out, ultimately the Heathrow north-west runway scheme was still selected as the best choice to tackle capacity issues in the south-east. 'When it was remodelled, the economic benefits just disappeared in a puff of smoke,' says Nic Ferriday, who wrote the Airports Watch analysis. 'It was extraordinary.'

The Airports National Policy Statement 2018

With the long-awaited conclusion to the Airports Commission process the government accepted the overarching principle of a need for extra runway capacity in the south-east. A year later, in October 2016 following further studies, it backed the choice of the north-west runway scheme. This runway was expected to be funded mostly by the private company that owns the airport, Heathrow Airport Holdings Limited, which would submit a planning application. The UK government would be responsible for supporting development of the public transport and possibly some of the road infrastructure necessary to handle larger numbers of passengers. It also had to create a regulatory and planning landscape that would allow Heathrow Airport to eventually apply for planning consent. One approach would be to draft a hybrid bill, under which Parliament would debate the need for the infrastructure and then vote on whether a proposed scheme should go ahead. This is how the HS2 works got under way. Another would be to designate a new National Policy Statement under the 2008 Planning Act.

As we saw in Chapter 1, before the introduction of the 2008 Planning Act the final decision on whether a major planning application would go ahead was based on the results of planning inquiries, which often had few terms of reference for how to make decisions about national infrastructure. The 2008 Act introduced a new development consent process for large infrastructure projects, which became known as Nationally Significant Infrastructure Projects (NSIPs); these might cover water and waste services, energy (nuclear, oil or gas), or ports, railways and airports. To create a clear framework for deciding on these projects, first the government would produce National Policy Statements for each area, which should form the basis for the Secretary of State's assessment of a scheme, unless it 'leads to the UK being in breach of its international obligations'. Crucially, and thanks to the hard work of groups such as FoE in lobbying during the consultation process leading up to the Act, there is now a legal requirement on the government to set out in these NPSs how the proposed policy will mitigate and adapt to climate change. The document is also expected to explain how the proposed project will contribute to sustainable development, as well as assessing the projections of demand and limitations on existing capacity.

Partly in response to the protracted length of the Terminal 5 Planning Inquiry, the new regulatory regime aimed to reduce the amount of time and paperwork necessary to get these large infrastructure projects agreed. Development Consent Orders would replace the need to seek separate consents.

Planning inspectors would still have a role to play in making recommendations to the government, but the ultimate decision for consent to go ahead now rests with the Secretary of State, who should make the decision based on the principles laid out in the relevant NPS.[19]

The National Policy Statement on aviation was one of the last to be drawn up, partly because of the uncertainty over the conclusion to the Airports Commission process. NPSs governing ports and energy infrastructure were designated by the coalition government in 2012 and 2011. Once the Airports Commission report was published in 2015, the path the government could follow to develop airport capacity through expansion was clear. A draft Airports NPS (ANPS) was drawn up in February 2017 and sent out for consultation, before Theresa May called a snap general election in a bid to silence her Brexit rivals. The ANPS explicitly accepted the case for airport expansion in the south-east and backed the new north-west runway as the preferred scheme. It outlined the regulatory hurdles to be overcome in order to make this a reality.

The document was subject to scrutiny from the House of Commons Transport Select Committee. In a report published in March 2018, the committee made twenty-five recommendations on how the ANPS could be improved, but essentially agreed with the government's assessment that more runway capacity was needed and that Heathrow was the obvious choice. Most of the recommendations surrounded the issues of local air pollution and noise, affordability, financing and compensation for affected communities. Expert witness testimony was presented on a day of hearings into the significant climate impacts of the expansion, including a submission from Lord Deben.[20]

In the 2017 election, Chris Grayling, MP for Epsom and Ewell, retained his seat, and position as Secretary of State for Transport, which he had held since 2016. Over the years Grayling had acquired the unfortunate nickname 'Failing Grayling' among more hostile elements of the press, a reference to a list of controversies during his time in office which had resulted in several of his decisions being brought into question. As justice secretary (2012–15) he pushed through a controversial privatisation programme for the probation service, which was overturned five years later after excessive costs and a reported increase in re-offending. In 2017 the Supreme Court ruled that new fees for employment tribunals that he had introduced in 2013 should be scrapped, and the Court of Appeal ruled against his cuts to legal aid on several occasions. As transport secretary he would go on to preside over botched changes to rail timetables which caused delays to millions of commuters, and to approve the issue of a £13.8m contract for post-Brexit ferries to a company that did not have any ferries, another decision which was quickly overturned.

One of the first things on Grayling's desk when the new Parliament opened in July 2017 was to put the ANPS forward for Parliamentary approval. The final ANPS was laid before the Commons for a ratifying vote on 26 June 2018. Although it involved a wider appraisal of the need to expand capacity in the aviation sector in general, it was hard not to see the document as associated only with supporting the principle of expansion in the south-east and laying down the conditions for the development of the 'government's preferred scheme' at Heathrow. On strategy, the document agreed with much of what the Commission had reported. In the early sections of the ANPS, much of the text seems to rerun the Commission's arguments for protecting Heathrow's global position as a hub airport, and its explanations why the Gatwick and extended Heathrow runway schemes were rejected. Although the north-west runway scheme would be the most expensive and have the highest carbon impact, it offered the best potential for maximising growth in flight destinations and passenger numbers and building the UK's global reputation.

The ANPS and Paris Agreement temperature limits

A key element of the ANPS which in June 2018 was presented to MPs to vote on was the conclusion that all three of the schemes analysed in the Airports Commission report 'can be delivered within the UK's obligations under the Climate Change Act 2008'.[21] Establishing whether this was correct was an important part of the Heathrow JR which is the subject of this book. So how were these conclusions reached?

It is difficult to analyse the ANPS modelling in any great detail, because the rules at the time it was drafted did not formally include aviation emissions in carbon budgets. They should be taken into account through leaving 'headroom', but there was no legal measure to ensure that this happened. There was an assumption that IAS *would* eventually be included before 2050 but, at this point, government policy was no more than the assumption that aviation emissions would be dealt with at the international level (i.e. through the EU ETS). Importantly for the Heathrow JR in coming years, this could be taken to imply that the emissions from the actual planes departing or arriving at an airport would not have to be included in calculating their impact on the domestic carbon budget.

One fact agreed ahead of the Heathrow JR was that the DfT had calculated that in a scenario with an expanded Heathrow, the total emissions from UK aviation in 2050 would be around 40MtCO2e – the figure we saw above. The ANPS modelling of how much it would cost to keep within the CCC's planning assumption of 37.5MtCO2e appears to have been based on the use of a series of indicative 'carbon values'. These assume that society places a monetary value on one tonne of carbon dioxide, a 'carbon abatement cost'. According to a report from The New Economics Foundation, the carbon abatement cost presented to Parliament and ministers at this time for the purposes of designating the ANPS was around £50bn.[22] Was this the correct figure? One former official with detailed knowledge of how these carbon budgets and costs are evaluated claims that the DfT modelling was done in a 'black box' independent of the BEIS decarbonisation strategy which was still being developed at that time.[23]

In addition, a lot of the difficulty in carbon budget modelling comes down to trying to determine whether any individual project is going to be the one to tip the UK's net carbon budget into the red. This was especially true when the target was 80% reduction, not Net Zero. As the backers of any one project could claim, their preferred scheme could go ahead as long as someone else made enough reduction somewhere else in the economy, leading to the phrase 'hiding in the twenty' (remaining 20% budget). In the context of the UK's total annual CO2 emissions of around 450MtCO2e, 40MtCO2e could be made to seem relatively minor. When trying to demonstrate that any one project would not tip the balance, any theoretical mix of carbon mitigation plans could be employed. For example, it might be plausible to argue that Heathrow expansion could go ahead if another million heat pumps were installed, or if another 10,000 hectares of forest were planted. In the economic modelling, this might involve pushing the carbon price lever upwards and upwards until the right answer was found. Decisions are 'not necessarily binary or rational', the former official told me.

It is not difficult to see how this may have influenced the job of deciding whether it would be possible to stay within carbon budgets – presumably the decision makers considered they only had to be satisfied that any increase in emissions above the planning assumption could be balanced across the whole UK's carbon budget by reductions in other economic sectors. Another crucial question was what temperature limit one was trying to achieve.

Remember that, at this point the UK's domestic obligations were based on CCA 08 (80% emissions reductions to limit global temperature rises to 2°C). It goes without saying that modelling to keep temperature rises below 2°C requires lower carbon abatement costs than modelling to keep temperature rises below 1.5°C.

What about the Paris Agreement? In reading the ANPS it seems quite clear that the 2°C target was the only benchmark against which the north-west runway project had been assessed. As the court process revealed, the Agreement was mentioned a couple of times in a consultation document, but there were no references to it in the final ANPS text. This did acknowledge that the government has 'international obligations', and that the Planning Act 2008 requires infrastructure projects not to 'lead the UK to be in breach of those commitments'. However, the only actual mention of 'Paris' was a statement that Charles de Gaulle Airport was challenging Heathrow's hub status. The

2015 Paris Agreement and its aspiration to limit temperature rises to 1.5°C, an achievement the UK claimed to be proud to have supported, was entirely absent from the text and references.

Securing a development consent order

The ANPS is the planning document which sets the overall policy direction for aviation. Any application for a development consent order to expand the airport is then subject to a secondary assessment whether it fits with the strategic objectives. The ANPS lays out a number of steps any developer needs to take in order to show it has considered mitigation for the negative impacts of an expansion. It lists out a number of areas – these include noise, habitats, air quality and surface access (roads and public transport) – where any potential developer needs to show it has taken meaningful steps to mitigate the negative impacts of both construction and operation of the new facility. A number of potential measures are outlined: for example being able to show that regular night flights would be ruled out, that concentration of flight paths could be avoided using new airspace routes, that waste material from construction is not contaminated and that Heathrow becomes a 'better neighbour' to local communities.

On carbon impacts, the document contains the key phrase:

Any increase in carbon emissions alone is not a reason to refuse development consent, unless the increase in carbon emissions resulting from the project is so significant that it would have a material impact on the ability of Government to meet its carbon reduction targets, including carbon budgets.[24]

How could a developer show that building a third runway and bringing in an extra quarter of a million planes annually would not lead to a breach of the UK's climate commitments? The key to this was the meaning of the term 'material impact', which would come back to haunt legal arguments during the Heathrow JR a year later. In 2018 it was unclear whether this meant the inclusion of carbon emissions from the actual planes in flight, which would make up around 95% of the total emitted from the newly expanded airport. The potential mitigation measures suggested in the ANPS are mostly steps that could be taken *at the airport*, such as reducing taxiing and emissions from aircraft waiting at departure gates, using low-emission vehicles at the airport and using low-carbon heating in airport buildings; or savings in operation such as encouraging at least 50% of staff and passengers to travel to the airport using public transport. The ANPS requires developers to take a number of steps including reporting on the projected carbon impact of the expansion and assessing greenhouse gas impacts before and after mitigation, but does not explicitly require the applicant to take responsibility for mitigating emissions from aircraft in flight, departing or arriving. Nor is there any mention of non-CO2 warming impacts of aviation.

Cait Hewitt from AEF believes that the exclusion of aviation emissions from domestic carbon budgets was key to understanding how Heathrow Airport planned to approach the mitigation of carbon emissions: 'The reason why Heathrow said a third runway wouldn't impact the UK's ability to achieve its carbon targets was that it was arguing that those targets did not apply to international aviation – only to emissions from the airport buildings and cars'.[25] Her argument is supported by Heathrow Airport's own consultation document on the third runway, from 2019:

> Our assessment has also considered carbon emissions in
> relation to UK policy and legislation on climate change.
> The carbon emissions from an expanded Heathrow are calcu-
> lated to be equivalent to 1.2% of the UK 2050 carbon target
> set by the Climate Change Act 2008. This comparison *excludes*
> [my emphasis] Greenhouse Gas emissions from international
> aviation, which are not included in current UK carbon budgets
> or explicitly in the UK's 2050 target. Heathrow's contribution
> to total emissions from international flights departing the UK in
> 2050 remains comparable to today. Expansion at Heathrow is
> not considered to materially affect the ability of the Government
> to meet UK carbon reduction targets.[26]

On 5 June 2018 Grayling briefed the House of Commons
about the upcoming vote to approve the ANPS. The official legal position remained the CCA 08 80% reduction/2°C
limit. In 2016, in response to the UK's signing of the Paris
Agreement the previous year, the CCC had recommended
that no further action to reflect the more ambitious temperature limits of the Agreement be taken until the 'carbon policy
gap' had been closed; in other words, the UK needed to hit
its already stretching targets before anything else could be
proposed. However, by 2018, it seemed that change might
be on the cards. A few months before Grayling's briefing,
the UK government had been given a draft copy of an IPCC
report which laid out in stark language the difference between
1.5°C and 2°C warming; and of course two-and-a-half years
had passed since the Paris Agreement. The claimants in the
Heathrow judicial review were convinced that the government
must have known that climate budgets would need to be tightened. Despite this, Grayling made no reference to either the
Climate Change Act or the Paris Agreement in his Commons
statement.

The CCC was beginning to find teeth. On 14 June, Lord Deben wrote to Grayling to express 'surprise' that his statement to Parliament had made no mention of CCA 08 or the Paris Agreement.[27] In polite language that perhaps belied the frustration behind it, Lord Deben again laid out the case that aviation was already projected to consume a large share of the UK's carbon budget; he went on 'higher levels of aviation emissions in 2050 must not be planned for, since this would place an unreasonably large burden on other sectors'.[28] Grayling replied to Lord Deben that he could not be expected to include 'every detail' in an oral statement to Parliament.

The Commons vote was also scheduled to take place a few days before the CCC published its 2018 progress report. This described how aviation emissions were increasing so fast that they would lead to carbon budgets in every other sector of the economy having to be tightened even further. Lord Deben repeated his assertion that aviation had to be kept within the 37.5MtCO2e limits, highlighting the DfT's own figures suggesting that Heathrow expansion would drive this figure to 39.9MtCO2e. *The Sunday Times* claimed that the vote had been scheduled deliberately to make it impossible for MPs to read and digest the CCC's new recommendations beforehand.[29]

In the days leading up to the Commons vote on the ANPS on Monday 25 June 2018, the debate became increasingly acrimonious. On one side was a significant chunk of the business community, unions representing workers at Heathrow, Labour MPs willing to disagree with their leader Jeremy Corbyn's rejection of the expansion and a majority of Conservative MPs who were likely to obey the party whip. On the other side were environmental campaigners, five west London councils, the Mayor of London Sadiq Khan, Labour members following their leader's line and eight Conservative MPs with west London constituencies who had vowed to block expansion. Mystery surrounded the whereabouts of foreign secretary Boris Johnson, who in 2015 announced to his constituents in Uxbridge and South Ruislip that he would 'lie down in front of the bulldozers' if the expansion ever went ahead. It eventually emerged that he had gone on an unannounced visit to Afghanistan, so would be a long way from the House of Commons when the vote took place. In contrast, four days before the vote Greg Hands, MP for Chelsea and Fulham, resigned his position as a junior minister for trade. Mr Hands announced that he was keeping his pre-election pledge to constituents. In a remarkable turnaround, eight years after the coalition prime minister David Cameron scrapped plans by a Labour government to expand Heathrow, his successor Theresa May gave her MPs a three-line whip to support Tory plans to expand Heathrow. Labour gave its MPs a free vote on the issue, mostly because the unions supported the job creation possibilities. The leadership of the party, Jeremy Corbyn and his deputy John McDonnell whose constituency Hayes and Harlington was right in the firing line of the new development, were against expansion.

As the MPs lined up to cast their vote in the Commons late that night, twelve protestors from the group Vote No Heathrow staged a 'lie-in' – a tactic which was becoming increasingly popular with environmental protestors and would become a signature of Extinction Rebellion protests later that year – in the lobby of the Commons. Security guards blocked the entrance doors as the group laid on the floor and chanted in a cheeky reference to Johnson's bulldozer pledge. In the Commons, shouts of 'Where's Boris?' were heard as the Tory rebels spoke out against the plans. It was all to no avail. The results came in at 10.17pm. The ANPS was passed and Heathrow expansion would go ahead. The yes vote secured a majority of 296 – 415 votes against 119 noes. Eight Conservative MPs had rebelled – Adam Afriyie, Sir David Amess, Bob Blackman, Zac Goldsmith, Justine Greening, Greg Hands, Matthew Offord and Theresa Villiers.

It was a bitter blow to those who opposed the plans. 'People simply get ignored in this process; you actually have to be either a big business or, I think, a big union before your voice counts, and that is totally unacceptable,' said Greening after the vote. Old arguments that Heathrow expansion was only a problem for London may have swung Labour MPs from elsewhere in the country to vote on what was promised to be an important bonus for the economy. Labour MP Helen Hayes, for West Norwood and Dulwich, who voted against the plans, told me that even in 2018 there was a clear distinction between MPs who were 'engaged' on climate, and those who were not. However, although a three-line whip had been imposed on Conservative MPs, the scale of the victory appeared surprisingly out of tune with a public debate that seemed to be moving quickly towards an appreciation of the serious challenges presented by climate change. To many, it just seemed wrong. In a powerful intervention, Labour's John McDonnell warned that an 'iconic, totemic' fight over climate change was about to be unleashed.

The ANPS was designated the next day, 26 June 2018.

THE PARIS AGREEMENT'S DAY IN COURT

The mood in the Friends of the Earth offices the day after the Commons vote was gloomy. FoE's new offices at the Printworks on Clapham Road in London, which replaced a crumbling building at Old Street, won a design award for sustainability when it was opened in 2014. Members of staff gathered in small groups in the treehouse, a raised area in the main meeting room decorated with forest pictures and comfy cushions. Others discussed the Commons vote in hushed tones in the break-out pods shaped like icebergs and boats, nursing takeaway oat milk flat whites (in a multitude of reusable cups) from the Italian café downstairs. Friends of the Earth had been campaigning against Heathrow expansion on and off since the 1990s, mostly through central support to the local west London group and characters such as Nic Ferriday. For some present that day it was hard to believe the story had come round again.

That morning, FoE's CEO Craig Bennett had travelled down to London from his home in Cambridge. 'I read the newspaper that morning and as I stared out of the train window it just struck me that I had to go and find our lawyers and see what we could do. It was obvious from the Commons vote that there was no real opposition to Heathrow expansion, so FoE would need to be HMG's official opposition on the environment.'[1]

Craig had long been thinking that FoE would have to consider mounting a challenge based on the CCA 08 legal targets. Bennett had worked at FoE in the 2000s when the Big Ask campaign had been at its height. For several years after the CCA was passed a number of backbench MPs had wanted to repeal it; Bennett said that had put him off the idea of a challenge at that time. But by 2017 it seemed that the CCA 08 was here to stay; 'having worked so hard to achieve that landmark legislation, it made sense that we would need to challenge it legally to understand what the legal community believed was compatible with reductions targets and what wasn't'.[2] When Bennett arrived at the Printworks that morning, he crossed from his glass office in the south wing in the hope that Will Rundle, an affable lawyer with a clipped brown beard, would be at his desk in the north wing. The office is a large, open-plan space so it was hard for Bennett to spot Will without attracting attention. He crouched down next to Will's desk; 'I asked him in a quiet voice if there was any chance that we could find a way to challenge the ANPS. Will's face changed colour, and there was a flicker of excitement. Within seconds we had a cheeky little conspiracy between us. It was like we couldn't not do it.'

Will remembers Craig crouching down beside his desk with a copy of the ANPS in his hand. 'Craig was outraged that for such a massive carbon intensive project there was no mention of the Paris Agreement at all,' recalls Will. 'I was delighted when he said this, because that was what I had signed up for! It's not often you get a single project that in and of itself has such a large climate impact.' Craig had identified even with a superficial read that the ANPS seemed to have been assessed against the outdated CCA 08 target. It was Will's job to try to prove this. He already knew it would be complicated, but agreed to talk to the rest of the legal and policy team at Friends of the Earth, and set up a meeting to look into potential arguments that could be put to the barristers.

Also watching the Commons vote had been Tim Crosland from Plan B. 'For me the decision was an opportunity,' says Crosland. 'We were specifically looking for cases which could test the legal significance of the Paris Agreement. Holding governments to account for their commitments to align to the 1.5°C limit, which is humanity's lifeline, was our purpose from the start.'[3] Crosland is a bespectacled lawyer with a close-cropped, greying beard. Five years previously he had founded his own organisation, Plan B Earth, after resigning from his job as a government lawyer. 'I went to Nigeria to negotiate on behalf of the UK government and people were telling me about the disaster of Lake Chad, the primary fresh-water resource for around 20 million people, which has lost most of its volume in the last few decades, with climate change a major cause. I just couldn't accept that I had been flown into a country whose people had contributed so little to the crisis, but were already suffering so badly, to provide advice on security measures, when everything my country was doing was driving insecurity, in Nigeria and internationally.' When I finally met Tim in person, a year after the coronavirus pandemic had forced all our exchanges onto Zoom, we met for an open-air coffee in a south London park. He'd just had his second dose of vaccine and I had barely spoken to anyone outside my immediate family for months, at least, not in person. I had too much caffeine, and we both struggled to remember the rules of a two-way conversation. 'I went to the Paris conference and then listened to the

UK Government's claims to the public that it had secured a landmark agreement to safeguard our future,' he told me excitedly. 'That's when I decided to set up Plan B Earth – to test the Government's sincerity.'[4]

Just a few months before the Commons vote, Crosland had attempted one of the first significant legal tests of the flagship CCA 08 in court. In late 2017, Plan B Earth issued a formal 'letter before legal action' asking the government to align its domestic target with the commitments in the Paris Agreement it had signed. Plan B, on behalf of eleven claimants 'from every walk of life', argued that the Paris Agreement had committed all signatories to pursuing efforts to keep warming to 1.5°C, and that the CCA 08 had been drawn up at a time when the real dangers of relying on the 2°C temperature limit had not been fully understood. The NGO argued that BEIS (or rather, its Secretary of State) had the power under section 2 of the CCA 08 to review the emissions reduction target in the light of the new commitment under the Paris Agreement. A draft copy of the IPCC report warning of the stark differences between a world 1.5°C warmer than pre-industrial levels, and one 2°C warmer, had been circulated to governments in early 2018. Plan B also wrote to the CCC urging it to review its 2016 recommendation to the government that this was not the correct time to review the 80% reduction target. In response, the CCC stated that the 80% reduction target was 'potentially consistent' with a range of temperature outcomes including the Paris 1.5°C commitment, and recommended against any action at that time.

This application for a JR ultimately failed. The High Court concluded that the Paris Agreement did not commit any country legally to any level of emissions reduction, and that the CCA 08 did not commit the Secretary of State to conducting a review, but only gave him powers to order one if he thought necessary. However, its decision to refuse the hearing came as the government did indeed commit to review the 80% reduction target in April 2018, which seems to have been in response to a request by the CCC.

Crosland had been inspired to go further and look for other cases after this outcome. 'The lesson, from our perspective, was that litigation could make things happen, whether inside or outside the court,' he said.[5] He felt sure that the political ground was moving, and he had a strong belief that at least behind the scenes there was a recognition that the 80% reduction would need to be revised in light of the dire warnings of the IPCC's twelve-year report. When this review was announced and the JR refused, Crosland believed that momentum was behind Plan B immediately launching another action against the designation of the ANPS. 'It was opportunistic, but that's how it should work,' he told me. 'We wanted to be fast, we never wanted to be bogged down by having to find funding; we just want to be agile.'

Strategic litigation

Strategic litigation is sometimes called impact litigation, and involves bringing a case with the goal of creating broader changes in society. The aim is to leave a lasting mark beyond the impact of a single case. In its most successful form, strategic litigation can be both an advocacy and regulatory strategy – confirming or clarifying how the law should be read and acting as an accountability mechanism. In the environmental movement there is a long tradition of these kinds of case, in the UK historically the preserve of the big and well-financed NGOs such as Friends of the Earth or Greenpeace.

The overall goal of strategic litigation is not so much to win one case, but to bring attention to an issue, build a narrative around it and try to create a significant precedent for future actions. 'If you do it right, it's about winning in the court of public opinion and pushing forward the debate,' says Bennett. It is also about creating real drama in that court – part of the goal in recent years has been increasingly to construct a narrative that will convince judges and the public of the necessity for acting before it is too late: 'litigants are shown to develop a notion of urgency for national climate policy with the help of symbols and discourses … in order to attribute meaning to complex models of future climate and the immediate responsibility of states to limit future warming,' writes Phillip Paiement.[6]

So just how do you go about this? The Heathrow JR was immensely complicated and involved four different teams working on separate issues and using different methods and approaches. Is it really as simple as Craig Bennett having an idea one morning on a train, and everyone in an organisation pulling together? Friends of the Earth had already had experience of harnessing a large part of an organisation to pull together on one campaign in the run-up to the designation of the CCA 08. This sometimes puts strain on teams who feel their work on other issues is being overlooked. In 2018, FoE was stretched to the limit with campaigns on fracking, pesticide use and bees, air pollution and road building; some in the organisation resisted the idea of returning to a single focus on climate change. Attacking flying was seen as toxic in some quarters as it ran the risk of making the organisation sound preachy, as if no-one would be allowed to go on holiday again.

At the same time, many campaigners feared they would lose supporters and donations from individuals if 'softer' environmental issues such as the nature campaign or the fight to save bees from pesticide use were wound up. By their very nature, legal challenges are complex; if you find the explanations of the case in this book difficult, you are not alone. For organisations reliant on foundations, corporate supporters and individual giving, serious thought needs to be dedicated to working out what people want their money spent on. It is a big job to create an overarching narrative of the importance of one particular court case – especially if there is a risk that it may fail. Heathrow had historically been seen as an issue that only affected the south of England; could it be turned into a David and Goliath battle that everyone in the UK should care about? Pete Lockley, a barrister who represented FoE in the case, says that the campaigners had one key advantage from the start: 'you know that a case about Heathrow will get lots of publicity because the press are always keen to run stories about the airport'.[7]

Organising these challenges takes a dedicated team of specialists. Big organisations such as Greenpeace and FoE have inhouse legal teams who can follow political developments, search for legal and political avenues and be responsible for engaging solicitors to help prepare the background to a case and advise on whether it is winnable. If the organisation feels it has a decent case and gets the go-ahead from the court, the final stage would be to employ a barrister or QC to argue the case. The loser usually pays the opposing side's legal costs, which can put off small groups considering whether to take on a government which will hire top barristers to argue its side. Of course, hiring a top QC is not cheap but these cases are often taken on by barristers on a *pro bono* basis as arguing a socially important case allows them to burnish their CV. In the Heathrow case, FoE partnered with the solicitor firm Leigh Day which rose to prominence in the 2000s after a number of campaigning human rights and environment cases in Africa. For instance, in 2006 Leigh Day sued the Dutch firm Trafigura which had dumped a ship-full of toxic waste in Ivory Coast where it was believed to be causing death and illness. The firm also brought a case against the British government calling for compensation for over 1,000 Kenyans who had been tortured in internment camps in Kenya during the Mau Mau uprising against colonial rule in the 1950s.

In recent years there has been a movement to throw off the shackles of what some have viewed as a cumbersome process. A number of new campaigning legal organisations have been established with the specific goal of taking on strategic litigation, particularly in the environmental field. Some have tried to set themselves up as one-stop shops where the entire organisation is dedicated to winning strategic litigation. They offer advantages: the organisation is specialised, and legal costs can be reduced by keeping everything in-house. Other organisations go broader, such as Uplift, established by climate lawyer Tessa Khan who worked on the *Urgenda* case in the Netherlands (see Chapter 5) and cofounded the Climate Litigation Network. Uplift is working on developing the movement towards a fossil-free UK, and aims to develop a narrative around strategic litigation which 'needs to be part of a broader advocacy strategy'. While it supports cases such as the Paid to Pollute JR, which is arguing against subsidies for oil and gas production, Khan argues that 'litigation needs to be part of a strategy. It's not enough to use it as a tactic.'[8]

Perhaps the most famous of these specialist organisations is Client Earth, set up in the UK in 2007 by James Thornton to use 'advocacy, litigation and research' to deal with climate change and nature loss. It was established as a charity to help it raise funds to cover the cost of cases; this meant it would not be beholden to fighting the more lucrative corporate cases. Client Earth has been described as a 'public interest law firm'. Arguably its most famous success was three successive court cases starting from 2011, which eventually found the UK government to have broken the law on levels of NO_2 air pollution. The judges in the cases ordered ministers to produce new, compliant, air quality plans to tackle the problem. The charity has gone on to establish offices in a number of countries where it fights local environmental cases.

Plan B, one of the claimants in the Heathrow case, is another example of how this new approach is developing. Tim Crosland set up the organisation and does most of the legal preparatory work himself, with a small team of volunteers who support when they can. They are not dependent on regular funding streams. Plan B seeks to challenge the traditional way of doing things. They do not use expert evidence in court, because this can so often end in a battle between rival experts.

Another example of these pioneering law firms is the Good Law Project. GLP was established as a legal not-for-profit, run by barrister Jolyon Maugham who was called to the bar in 2015 after a pupillage at Lord Irving's chambers. Maugham rose to prominence after he argued a number of cases about Brexit and the prorogation of Parliament. GLP relies on personal donations and crowd-funding to operate, often running funding campaigns attached to specific legal cases as they happen. This means that people can make one-off donations if a particular case inspires them. It takes on a number of different public interest cases, only some of which are environmental. GLP hit the headlines in 2021 with a string of cases which investigated the way in which government contracts were awarded during the coronavirus pandemic and established that ministers Matt Hancock and Michael Gove had broken the law by not publishing contracts within the requisite period. It has begun to break into environmental cases over the last year, working on the early stages of legal challenges into air pollution and, as we will see below, expansion of Heathrow Airport.

Organisations such as GLP and Plan B are trying to upend the traditional way of doing things. Tim Crosland chooses not to use QCs, barristers or legal firms, preparing and arguing the cases himself. GLP seems to see virtue in a constant string of threats of legal action, some of which never make it past the initial letter of intent to request a JR. As we will see there are distinct advantages to operating in these new ways, much to do with the ability to be nimble and quick, and to not have to rely on getting funding from donors or regular supporters who may not want the NGO to take on a particular case. Smaller, innovative organisations do not have to wait to prepare cases until staff can be redeployed from other work.

However, there are also disadvantages to this newer approach. There is an enormous amount of paperwork to be completed, particularly gathering together court documentation for planning JRs. In these cases, applicants for a JR hearing are given just six weeks to put in their initial pre-action protocol letter. Other issues include the danger that individual lawyers with differing attitudes to risk will choose to pursue cases which others may think fanciful. There is an unwritten agreement between environmental lawyers that the movement should decide collectively which cases have a good chance of winning, particularly as a significant loss could close the door on other groups bringing challenges on the same grounds. This approach was somewhat tested in the enormous Heathrow JR where coordination between all the competing claims was not always as smooth as it could have been. Friends of the Earth and Plan B were just two of ten individual claimant groups. The groups came together on four separate claims which covered twenty-two individual grounds. The groups decided to proceed together, but their aims were not the same. FoE and Greenpeace both used inhouse lawyers to draft the first ideas for the case, then engaged firms of solicitors to help gather the paperwork and finally brought in a team of barristers to prepare the court arguments. There were two one-man-bands, Tim Crosland of Plan B and Neil Spurrier who acted as a litigant in person on behalf of the residents' pressure group Teddington Action Group. The Hillingdon claimants and the mayor's office used a barrister and a firm of solicitors. The Hillingdon, Spurrier and London Mayor claims focused on more traditional issues – air pollution, traffic congestion, habitat destruction and noise disturbance. Neil Spurrier, who was the first to issue his claim, included a climate change ground and a ground of conflict of interest (since Howard Davies had previously advised the Singapore Investment Corporation, one of Heathrow Airport's shareholders). In order to simplify, the High Court heard Spurrier's climate ground jointly with the climate arguments of Plan B and FoE. As we shall see these claims were more entangled, more innovative and some would say risky, and we shall also see that they did not always complement one another. There was some tension between Tim

Crosland's desire to break the mould and Friends of the Earth's desire to play safe for a winnable case based on its many years of experience in strategic litigation.

Managing the expectations of campaign groups and donors is another issue. Individuals who feel passionately about a particular cause and contribute to a crowd-funder in the expectation of a court case may be disappointed if the claim goes nowhere. Similarly, small community groups may be left disappointed if their cause is taken on by a legal charity but goes nowhere. For example, GLP contacted a number of small air-pollution campaign groups in 2020, asking whether they would put their name to a pre-action protocol letter asking for a review of the government's air pollution strategy in the light of evidence that dirty air is connected to the occurrence and severity of coronavirus infections. The case rested on the precautionary principle, that the government should act to improve air quality even if the link had not been conclusively proved. However, the legal action went nowhere, and a number of the claimants contacted by the GLP were left disappointed.

Judicial review

In the UK, the only legal avenue available to campaigners wishing to challenge government decisions is a judicial review. It is an option used by many environmental and social justice campaigners to attempt to challenge government decision-making. JR is a procedure that allows anyone who has been affected by a decision or a failure to act by a public authority to apply to the courts to rule whether these actions or inactions were lawful. Judicial reviews do not concern themselves with the merits of the decision – whether or not it was the right thing to do – merely whether the law as it stood at the time was correctly followed when the decision was made. This means that JR can be a limited tool as it takes no account of the political or moral climate around a particular decision. 'Sometimes the cases are on very basic points of law, but often lawyers have to be innovative or creative, performing gymnastics, when drawing up a JR challenge,' says Joana Setzer, assistant professor in climate change and governance at LSE.[9] JR is seen as an essential part of defending the principle of Parliamentary sovereignty – laws made by Parliament cannot be overruled by the judiciary. Challenges are only allowed against executive decisions, to ensure that the decision has been made in accordance with law created by Parliament.

A JR claim can challenge any public body – ministers, local authorities, government departments and bodies such as the Environment Agency. A group needs to show that it has 'standing' before it can make a claim, which means demonstrating that it has been affected by the decision in some way. This can be difficult in environmental cases, because by definition such cases affect everyone and no-one in particular. Individuals can make a claim for judicial review and represent themselves, but a significant number of cases are brought by campaign groups in particular policy areas, which may look for a legal firm and/or barrister with experience in JR to act on their behalf.

The first step in a JR is to send a pre-action protocol letter to the body to be reviewed; if the response is inadequate, a claim for JR can be lodged at the High Court. There is time pressure on this process – in planning cases, such as the Airports ANPS challenge, the claim must be lodged within six weeks of the decision being made; in other cases the time limit is three months. This makes a JR claim challenging for inexperienced campaign groups who may not fully understand the process of putting together a convincing case. The documentation alone is a major headache. Once this is ready, the initial claim is then presented to a judge who decides whether the case is arguable, a step which weeds out cases where it is difficult to see where the error of law has occurred. These requirements mean that only about 5% of cases are approved to move on to the next stage, a full hearing.

There are three main grounds on which a decision can be overturned – illegality (if the person making the decision did not have authority to make it), procedural unfairness (if the decision was improper) and irrationality (that no reasonable person would make that decision). If the claimant wins this substantive case, the government decision in question can be quashed, or declared unlawful. In some cases, the decision will need to be made again (and in fact the same conclusion might be reached, but via a better process); in others, the court may order the government or public body to provide a specified remedy.[10] Appeals are allowed under the system, and will initially be heard by the Court of Appeal; a further appeal to the Supreme Court is sometimes allowed, but there the decision is final.

Along with this intimidating timeline, cost is another major obstacle to JR. Campaigners are often put off by the rule that the loser pays the winner's costs, as well as their own. However, environmental claimants are protected to some extent because the UK is party to the Aarhus Convention, an agreement signed in 1998 which grants the public rights to participate in and seek justice on governmental decisions on matters concerning the environment. Aarhus provides cost protection to environmental claimants – individual costs are limited to £5,000 and community or campaign group costs to £10,000. The government attempted to change these rules in 2017, although FoE and the RSPB jointly challenged this in a largely successful judicial review. In practice, many community groups now use crowd-funding platforms to raise money towards the cost of a JR, with the legal teams often acting *pro bono*.

JR as a process has increasingly come under the spotlight following two serious setbacks for the government in the Brexit process. Campaigner Gina Miller successfully argued in 2016 that Article 50 on exiting the European Union could only be invoked by Parliament, not by the government. Nearly three years later, she won again in a JR which established at the Supreme Court that the decision to prorogue Parliament in order to force through a no-deal Brexit in September 2019 had been unconstitutional. In what was widely viewed as a response to these challenges, the Conservative government elected in late 2019 committed in its manifesto to conduct a review of JR. The manifesto commitment argued that the system was being abused by too many claims which would never be successful and were merely being launched to hold up government policy making. The impacts of this review will be discussed in Chapter 5.

Building the case

We will now turn to how the legal arguments for a judicial review into the ANPS were constructed. The focus of this section is on what Plan B and FoE claimed would be the climate change impacts of the third runway plans. A number of other claims led to what was known as the 'rolled up' hearing at the High Court in March 2019, which I will briefly summarise.

The Hillingdon claimants

The Hillingdon group, as they became known, were a coalition of London local authorities which had worked together opposing airport expansion in all its various shapes and forms over twenty years. This group included Hillingdon, Richmond upon Thames, Hammersmith and Fulham, Wandsworth and Windsor and Maidenhead councils, areas significantly affected by aviation noise, airport traffic and the associated high levels of air pollution. This group was supported by the Mayor of London, Sadiq Khan, exercising his responsibility for Greater London's action on climate change, and the campaign group Greenpeace. Their argument was mostly based on the grounds of air pollution, home demolition and increased traffic volume which had become familiar in previous claims against Heathrow expansion. The Hillingdon plaintiffs' case focused on the argument that the Secretary of State had not carried out his duty to produce an adequate environmental report; for example, they argued that the use of indicative flight paths meant that communities were left in the dark about whether they would be affected by an increase in aircraft overflying in future. They argued that the AC had not taken into account all traffic modelling predictions, such as induced demand, and that the minister had ignored information submitted to the consultation by the London mayor about problems with roads, rail and surface access.[11]

A further argument was launched by Neil Spurrier on behalf of the Teddington Action Group. He focused on the government's air pollution provisions, in particular the emissions of NO_2 and particulate matter from planes and how these might breach legal limits. These two pollutants are highly dangerous, and have been linked with a number of respiratory conditions, heart and lung disease, dementia, miscarriage, stunted lung development in children and teenage psychotic episodes. Spurrier challenged the DfT's use of modelling that suggested that the effects of air pollution from planes were mostly confined to a radius of 2km around the airport. He argued that modelling from King's College London showed that the impacts of particulate matter from planes arriving and departing from Heathrow could be detected up to 40km from the airport.

A final challenge came from the competitors to the north-west runway scheme, Heathrow Hub Limited and Runway Innovations Limited. The HHL challenge was on behalf of Jock Lowe's proposed scheme to extend the existing runway, which had been rejected in the Airports Commission final report. In addition to all this, Heathrow Airport and Arora Group, a hotel and property company, appeared as interested parties in support of the ANPS. Arora Group hoped to ensure that competition provisions of the ANPS were maintained in order to allow it to produce a rival bid for the development of a proposed new terminal and hotel building at an expanded Heathrow.

The CO2 argument

Challenging Heathrow expansion on climate grounds was always going to be risky. Partly because neither CCA 08 nor the Paris Agreement specifically mention emissions from aviation and partly because, at the time the JR was launched in 2018, emissions from IAS were not formally included in the UK's carbon budgets, any legal challenge based on climate grounds would be difficult. The Paris Agreement sets no legally binding emissions reduction targets, and in any case in the UK domestic statute takes precedence over international treaties. The only legally binding aspect of Paris is a country's duty to produce an NDC every five years. If countries fail to meet their objectives, they face no penalties other than naming and shaming by other countries which may have been more successful. Previous legal challenges against the expansion at Heathrow had relied on the more established grounds of air pollution, habitat destruction and noise, which have basis in UK domestic law. I have heard that the CEO of another big environmental NGO told Craig Bennett that he was 'living in cloud cuckoo land' if he thought Heathrow could be defeated on climate grounds.

The policy position at the time seemed clear. As we have seen, both the Airports Commission and the ANPS stated that the plans for expanding the airport would not lead to the UK breaching its emissions reduction responsibilities. There may have been some dubious accounting, but could it be shown that the decision was taken without proper reference to the law, the test of a JR? 'Many lawyers chose not to bring cases on the Paris Agreement because it is risky,' Joana Setzer told me. 'Only the requirement to submit an NDC is legally enforceable. Lawyers will look for an easier route.'[12]

But many lawyers enjoy a challenge. The two main NGOs working on the request for a JR started to develop arguments to show that increasing the capacity of such a huge airport during a climate crisis would breach the UK's climate commitments and should not be allowed to proceed. FoE's challenge would eventually be based on the 2008 Planning Act; Plan B Earth homed in on whether a commitment to the Paris Agreement's 1.5°C temperature limit could be considered government policy.

Immediately after his cheeky and exciting conversation with Craig Bennett, Will Rundle began a conversation with Leigh Day to test some of his ideas for the shape of a possible JR claim. He spoke to solicitor Rowan Smith, a specialist in human rights and environmental JR cases, who had joined the firm in 2016. Rowan had previously worked with David Wolfe QC from Matrix Chambers, 'one of the best environmental public lawyers' and someone who had worked with FoE before, on fracking cases. Pete Lockley from 11 KBW chambers joined as the junior counsel; he was a former aviation campaigner turned barrister. It was very much a team effort. 'We quickly realised that we could focus on section 10 of the Planning Act, because we could see the ANPS did not mention the Paris Agreement,' says Rowan Smith.[13] At Friends of the Earth, Will worked with Katie de Kauwe to research the claim, with the help of a dedicated group of legal interns who helped to produce briefings, attended hearings and researched *Hansard*.[14]

Will adds that 'because of previous campaign work in the planning team when the Planning Act was made alongside the Climate Change Act 2008, I knew of the amendments we had won to the act to consider climate change and so I directed our focus onto that to develop a case based on it.'[15]

In parallel, Tim Crosland started to look for a complementary argument for his own claim. It was just a few weeks since his previous case had failed; he knew he would need to find another line of attack. The Planning Act seemed to him the obvious place to look. Tim's quick reading of the ANPS also convinced him there would be grounds for a legal challenge.

Despite the vastness of the Heathrow project, and what the campaigners passionately believed would be its huge impact on the UK's carbon emissions, developing the case was more like searching for a tiny needle in a large haystack. Every word and letter of the ANPS and the Planning Act had to be dug over, looking for clues which could withstand a defence lawyer's argument. The FoE team had to work hard to shape Craig Bennett's observation that Paris was absent from the text into a firm case. 'As someone who cares about climate change you just want to walk into the courtroom and say it's ridiculous, you can't expand a runway in a climate emergency!' says Pete Lockley. 'But as a lawyer you know what it actually comes down to is painstaking research and arguing very detailed legal and technical points.'[16]

Rushing against the clock to lay the groundwork to support their claim, the lawyers sent the pre-action protocol letter just before the six-week deadline was up, and sat tight for a tense wait. This was their one chance to try to persuade the court that the claim had merit. A few weeks later the reply came back. 'When the government replied to our pre-action protocol letter, we identified several gaps in its proposed defence,' says Rowan Smith.[17] The game was on. The claimants were given permission to move to a full hearing.

Major changes in the global understanding of the implications of apparently small differences between average temperature rises were occurring in 2018, partly due to the IPCC report. This had shown that in order to limit temperature rises to 1.5°C, Net Zero emissions needed to be achieved by 2050 at the latest, and even this would give only around a 50% chance that the climate could be stabilised. The claimants believed that if Paris *had* been considered in the modelling of how much CO_2 would be emitted from a new third runway at Heathrow, it should have been obvious that the project could not go ahead. The third runway was expected to contribute to the UK aviation sector's emissions rising to around 40MtCO2e by mid-century – and it was far from clear how Net Zero might be achieved. Plan B believed that in drawing up the ANPS, Chris Grayling had assessed the third runway's future climate impacts against a 2°C temperature limit, and not against Paris' ambitious 1.5°C limit. The climate claimants believed that the Secretary of State had erred in his decision by failing to consider Paris (an international commitment), as the law required. By extension it seemed that the carbon costs of mitigation in order to hit the 1.5°C limit, if properly assessed, would be extremely high, bringing into question the results of the cost–benefit analysis in the original ANPS supporting documents.

The challenges on climate grounds that the campaigners eventually settled on rested *not* on the flagship CCA 08, but on two pillars of the rather more humble 2008 Planning Act. Plan B's challenge rested on the line: 'The Planning Act 2008 requires that a national policy statement must give reasons for the policy set out in the statement and an explanation of how the policy set out in the statement takes account of Government policy relating to the mitigation of, and adaptation to, climate change'. Plan B argued that, when the ANPS was designated, government policy was already directed at achieving the aims of the Paris Agreement which the UK had ratified in 2016.

Friends of the Earth also chose to rely on the wider sustainability elements of the Planning Act. The NGO argued that the requirement to consider new infrastructure projects and draw up an NPS with sustainable development principles in mind meant that that the minister's duty was much broader, and required him to consider the entire landscape including international climate change agreements. This meant that he must consider the most important international climate change agreement that existed at the time the ANPS was designated – the Paris Agreement. In particular, the team homed in on how increased GHG emissions from Heathrow expansion meant it could not be described as a sustainable development as it would jeopardise the ability of future generations to 'meet their needs' (the 'Brundtland' definition of sustainable development – see Chapter 1).

Climate claims in detail

Plan B's argument rested on section 5(8) of the 2008 Planning Act:

> The reasons must (in particular) include an explanation of how the policy set out in the statement takes account of Government policy relating to the mitigation of, and adaptation to, climate change.

Tim Crosland's work involved collecting a substantial number of freely available official documents and Parliamentary statements, which he argued both demonstrated a clear commitment to achieving the aims of the Paris Agreement in the preceding years, and constituted government policy. For instance, he highlighted key sections of the 2017 Clean Growth Strategy drawn up by the Department of Business and Industrial Strategy,[18] which had taken on responsibility for climate policy. The Strategy made a number of clear references to both the UK's key role in securing the Paris Agreement, and the government's continued commitment to pursuing the Agreement's aims. Crosland also collected official statements by cabinet ministers Amber Rudd and Andrea Leadsom. In 2016, two years before the designation of the ANPS, Leadsom had said in Parliament 'the Government believe we will need to take the step of enshrining the Paris goal of net zero emissions in UK law'. A few days later, Amber Rudd, then Secretary of State for Energy and Climate Change had said, in response to a Parliamentary question, 'the Government will take the step of enshrining into UK law the long-term goal of net zero emissions, which I agreed in Paris last December'.

Crosland argued that these documents made it clear that in 2016, two years before the Commons vote paving the way for the third runway, the government had recognised that a fundamental shift in climate obligations was needed to meet the goals of the Paris Agreement. He concluded this met the requirements of the 'Government policy' statement in section 5(8). He argued that by 2018, when the ANPS was designated, science had made it abundantly clear that the 2°C limit was dangerously high. Moreover, by early 2018, well in advance of the Commons vote to designate the ANPS, governments around the world had been given an advance copy of the official publication of the IPCC's 'twelve-year' report which made the difference between a 1.5°C world and a 2°C world abundantly clear. Crosland argued that officials must have understood that change was coming, yet there was evidence that, in drawing up the ANPS, officials at the DfT, advising Grayling, had used the 2°C limit as a basis for assessing to what extent the Heathrow third runway would eat up the carbon budget allotted by the CCC. 'I started the case with the hypothesis that the government *knew* the figures didn't add up,' he told me. 'How could they? They *knew* that with expansion, emissions from UK aviation would increase. As part of the Paris commitment, emissions were supposed to be Net

Zero by the latter half of the century. We knew that Heathrow would lead to emissions from UK aviation alone still being 40MtCO2e in 2050. This is not Net Zero, however you look at it.'[19]

Friends of the Earth's approach rested on section 10 of the Planning Act 2008, which covered sustainable development:

(2) The Secretary of State must, in exercising those functions, do so with the objective of contributing to the achievement of sustainable development;

(3) For the purposes of (2) the Secretary of State must (in particular) have regard to the desirability of –
(a) mitigating, and adapting to, climate change ...

Section 10 is a much broader requirement than the section 5 CCA requirement to explain how the policy relates to the mitigation of climate change. To meet the section 10 requirement, the Secretary of State needs to show consideration of sustainable development as well as the policy requirement. FoE developed the argument that to meet this requirement, it was insufficient to rely only on the provisions of CCA 08, and that there was a broader duty on the minister concerned to consider deeper requirements. The second pillar of their argument was that aviation produces additional non-CO2 emissions, with scientific evidence suggesting that these effectively double aviation's warming impact.

Friends of the Earth worked with Rowan Smith and Leigh Day to build a case and prepare the court documents. David Wolfe and Pete Lockley were engaged early on to help shape thinking. 'David Wolfe focused on section 10 very quickly. He saw an opportunity from previous cases he'd worked on. It quickly became our key idea,' says Rowan Smith.[20] Wolfe and the team developed an argument that the Secretary of State had an obligation to take into account the ability of future generations to meet their needs when making decisions on designating NPSs, which includes taking into account international agreements such as the Paris Agreement and the underlying science of climate change.[21] Like Crosland, the team felt that by the time the ANPS was designated in 2018, the minister must have already been made aware of the upcoming public release of the IPCC twelve-years report with its warnings. The team believed that by the time the ANPS was designated in 2018, it was becoming obvious that the UK's 80% reduction target under CCA 08 might need to change.

The FoE argument also focused on the fact that the expanded Heathrow would be expected to remain a high carbon emitter well past 2050, at a time when other sectors of the UK economy should be expected to have reached Net Zero. This would compromise the ability of future generations to meet their needs, argued FoE, as these emissions would still need to be mitigated after other sectors had decarbonised. A further point was that, for the purposes of the ANPS, the economic benefits of Heathrow expansion had been assessed up to 2085, but not the climate or carbon impacts. FoE argued that by choosing to assess the ANPS against the CCA 08, which set climate targets only up to 2050, the Secretary of State had again breached his section 10 duty: 'climate change will not just stop in 2050,' said the FoE trial briefing documents.[22]

As the case documents were being compiled, a new lawyer joined Friends of the Earth. Katie de Kauwe was a couple of years into her practice, having studied biology and then taken a law conversion course at Bristol University. 'I had always wanted a career that would enable me to help protect the planet,' she told me. It was the first time Katie had been at such close quarters to a case being prepared at high speed. She threw herself into the research. Her scientific background helped her to focus on the non-CO_2 warming impacts of aviation. We have seen there is clear evidence that these cause two or three times as much warming as the CO_2 that aviation emits. Nitrogen oxides, sulphur and water vapour interact in complex ways with atmospheric chemistry at high altitudes, stimulating radiative forcing. While the FoE team had already picked up on the importance of considering these extra climate impacts, Katie started to wonder whether a ground could be based on the precautionary principle. This is a legal concept, often used in environmental cases, which recognises that delaying action on a possible threat because of uncertainty until compelling evidence of harm can be found will often mean that is it then too late to rectify the harm.

The final element of the FoE case rested on the failure to draw up the SEA for the ANPS correctly by considering Paris.

FoE also developed a number of smaller points which attempted to clarify the meaning of parts of the ANPS. These arguments were effectively clarified in the High Court case and did not proceed to appeal. The first was that the minister had failed his section 5 requirement to explain adequately how the relationship between the ANPS and the granting of any DCO would work. The team circled in paragraph 5.82:

> Any increase in carbon emissions alone is not a reason to refuse development consent, unless the increase in carbon emissions resulting from the project is so significant that it would have a

material impact on the ability of Government to meet its carbon
reduction targets, including carbon budgets.

What did the term 'material impact' really mean? FoE argued
that the ANPS text was not clear. For example, the team
believed the ANPS was not clear whether emissions from aircraft in flight (which make up around 95% of the emissions
from Heathrow) were to be covered by the DCO application
process, or just emissions from the building and construction
phase of the expansion. As we saw earlier, the suggested mitigation measures listed appear restricted to matters involving the
operation of the building, public transport and aircraft emissions on the tarmac. The ANPS stated that it was expected
that, over time, aircraft would develop to reduce harmful emissions, but that the developer was not directly responsible for
ensuring this.

Friends of the Earth also argued that the ANPS was not
sufficiently clear on *which* carbon targets should be used –
would they be the targets agreed when the ANPS was designated, which of course in 2018 was still 80% reduction by 2050,
or should they be the targets at the point that the application
for a DCO was submitted? In effect, would the carbon target
be 'frozen' at the point that the ANPS was designated? This
was crucial, because by early 2019 the IPCC's twelve-year
report had made it abundantly clear that nothing short of Net
Zero would succeed in stabilising global temperatures at no
more than 1.5°C above pre-industrial times. Less than a year
after the ANPS was designated, the CCA 08 targets did in fact
change: Net Zero became the new law. Part of the impetus
behind the case was to 'hold the line' on airport expansion until
those new commitments became reality.

The High Court case, March 2019

The campaigners' case got off to a good start. As Rowan Smith had suggested, the government's reply to their initial pre-action protocol letter made them suspect there was something encouraging in their line of argument.

The pre-trial hearing provided a tantalising glimpse of what was to come. In a surprising move, the Department for Transport conceded very early in the process that it *had indeed* used the old 80% reduction target to assess the climate impacts of the new runway. This concurred with the final published ANPS document, which as we have seen makes no mention of the Paris Agreement. This was something of a surprise to some of the legal teams, who had expected that the government might try a different argument, perhaps along the lines that the decision maker had taken Paris into consideration and had decided that it would not have made a difference to the final decision to designate the ANPS.

Ahead of the hearing, the government had been required to disclose all documents relevant to how the decision that the third runway plan would not compromise the UK's climate obligations had been made, including economic modelling of the carbon cost, and any different values used to analyse the impact on constraining emissions. The disclosure requested all documents covering what the decision maker knew and considered about the Paris Agreement target. This prompted a witness statement from Caroline Low, director of the Airport Capacity Programme at the DfT during the time that the ANPS was being drawn up, which made it plain that the Department had used the CCA 08 target as the basis for their assessments. Sitting in court, Tim Crosland says hearing this statement read out was the moment that he knew he was on solid ground: 'It was a lightbulb moment. This was when it all made intellectual sense to me.' The statement read:

> In October 2016 the CCC said that the Paris Agreement 'is more ambitious than both the ambition underpinning the UK 2050 target and previous international agreements' but that the UK should not set new UK emissions targets now, as it already has stretching targets and achieving them will be a positive contribution to global climate action. Furthermore, the CCC acknowledged in the context of separate legal action brought by Plan B against the Secretary of State for Business, Energy and Industrial Strategy that it is possible that the existing 2050 target could be consistent with the temperature stabilization goals set out in the Paris Agreement. Subsequently, in establishing its carbon obligations for the purpose of assessing the impact of airport expansion, my team has followed this advice and considered existing domestic legal obligations as the correct basis for assessing the carbon impact of the project, and that it is not appropriate at this stage for the government to consider any other possible targets that could arise through the Paris Agreement.[23]

It was as clear as the campaigners could have hoped for. The DfT officials *had* used the old 2°C limit under CCA 08 to assess the carbon impact of the project. Government lawyers had advised the Secretary of State that it was 'not appropriate' for him to consider other possible targets under Paris, because the provisions of the CCA 08 were sufficient and 'potentially consistent' with a range of temperature outcomes. Representing the government in this pre-trial hearing, James Maurici QC had to answer some tough questions. In the initial submissions, Maurici (who has a background in high-profile planning cases) had intimated that the government's line would be that

Grayling *had* considered Paris, and then used his discretion to decide that it should carry no weight. But in a surprise move Maurici explained in the pre-trial hearing that the legal advice had in fact been that the Paris Agreement was 'not relevant' – a legal term which means needing to be discounted. This was something that had not been raised in earlier proceedings. Tim Crosland recalls the drama in court:

> I remember the moment vividly. ... [R]aising his eyebrows, Mr Justice Holgate said, 'Mr Maurici … if not relevant, unlawful to take it into account?' 'Yes M'Lud.' (There was shock). Mr Maurici continued, 'As an unincorporated Treaty, it was not legally binding'.

Mr Justice Holgate became a QC in 1997 and was appointed to the Queen's Bench in 2014. He is known to lawyers as a judge who pays attention to detail and rigour, and was reportedly frustrated by this last-minute change. He required Mr Maurici to amend his pleadings accordingly. This is a formal legal process which means correcting his original pleadings using red ink. When the Divisional Court opened for the full hearing in March 2019, Maurici's argument was now that Paris, due to its status as an unincorporated treaty, was in fact 'not relevant' and therefore it would not have been legal to take it into account.

Leaving court that morning, Pete Lockley and David Wolfe walked together down the Strand, discussing what had happened. Their mood was buoyant. With this clarification, Wolfe believed that the case was crystallising around a key legal point which could be argued in court. The case was 'crisping up nicely'.

With what seemed like a killer piece of evidence of disagreements, the campaigners were confident going into the JR hearing. It had been an exhausting few weeks, gathering last-minute papers and ironing out discrepancies and policy arguments. Tim Crosland had wanted Friends of the Earth to commit to supporting his argument about government policy under section 5 in court, but they were proving reluctant. David Wolfe felt that it would be difficult to defend that position when it is generally established that domestic statute is the basis of government policy. FoE's press team were struggling to find a coherent message that worked for everyone, exchanging frustrating phone calls between all the respective claimant teams.

The hearing would last two weeks. It was to take place at the Royal Courts of Justice on the Strand and was scheduled to start on 11 March 2019, just four days before a planned youth climate strike that would turn out to be the biggest ever. Greta Thunberg and fellow campaigners from Fridays for Future called on young people across the world to skip classes and protest at the failure of leaders to properly address climate breakdown. After years of foot-dragging on climate, campaigners suddenly found the mood really seeming to change in early 2019. At that point, there were almost too many protests to go to. It was an extraordinary moment where climate campaigning seemed to take off and suddenly it seemed possible to talk about the lack of global action with people outside the environmental activist scene. For some, it was a replay of another moment in the late 2000s when it had seemed action on climate was coming together, but this time round a new generation of activists was coming of age. Concern about the effects of climate change seemed to be becoming mainstream, no longer a topic that elicited uncomfortable laughs and defensive justifications at dinner parties. For a few weeks the FoE office was half-empty as staff went to support the young people on climate strike and other rallies. On the morning the High Court case opened, a few faithful 'FoEsters' set off to the Strand, bearing green placards reading 'No climate-wrecking third runway'. On the steps of the court, they met campaigners from No Third Runway Coalition, Stop Heathrow Expansion, Plan B, Greenpeace and others. John McDonnell, the Labour shadow chancellor, whose Hayes and Harlington constituency sat directly under the Heathrow flightpath, stood with the Richmond Park MP Zac Goldsmith (Conservative).

When the campaigners got into the court, it was packed. The government legal team was large, led by James Maurici and two junior barristers. For the climate lawyers, it seemed a bit of a David and Goliath moment. The case was heard by Lord Justice Hickinbottom, a former solicitor who had been appointed to the Queen's Bench in 2009, and Mr Justice Holgate. The pace was slow as each of the four separate JR claims was explored. The judges were presented with a mountain of background documents. This involved folders of expert evidence on the various scientific aspects of the claims – for example, Tim Johnson of the AEF had been asked by FoE to provide a briefing about the complex non-CO_2 climate impacts of aviation, and the Tyndall Centre had prepared a report on the IPCC and the difference between 1.5°C and 2°C warming. In the pre-trial hearing Holgate had declared that there was so much material to wade through that it was a waste of time to try to decide whether all twenty-two claims should be given permission to proceed. He and Lord Justice Hickinbottom decided that all the claims should be heard together, which meant some of the grounds from individual claimants were not taken up.

As the court ploughed through four days of evidence, things began to hot up outside.

The politics of UK Net Zero

The UK's official political position on Net Zero seemed slow to catch up with the science. As we have seen, the government's view on carbon budgets, as required by the CCA 08, is informed by independent scientific advice provided by the Climate Change Committee. As late as 2016, as the draft ANPS was being drawn up, the CCC continued to advise the government that it was not the right time to legislate a Net Zero target. The advice had been produced in response to a subclause in the Paris Agreement committing signatory countries to 'pursue efforts to keep temperature rises to 1.5C'. In its October 2016 report on the UK's climate action following the Paris Agreement, the Committee argued that it was not yet the right time to act. It said that there were few global pathways anywhere for holding temperatures to the 1.5°C limit. Instead, the CCC concluded that the CCA 08 target should remain the basis of UK action. It served the recommendation with a dose of realism, estimating that the current policy was already insufficient to meet even the existing carbon budgets, and that the 'carbon policy gap must be closed' before even more stretching targets were designated.[24] This may have been a position of caution that the CCC came to regret, but in 2016 it meant that, for the UK government, the pain of legislating for Net Zero could be put off for another three years.

Youth Strike for Climate and Extinction Rebellion

However, the young people were not willing to wait. By 2019, the clamour for action on climate was growing deafening. Two movements played an important role in pushing climate change to national attention. The first was Youth Strike for Climate, or Fridays for Future, which was started by the Swedish activist Greta Thunberg. In August 2018, just two months after the MPs in the UK had voted through the Heathrow expansion, Thunberg began a sit-in strike outside the Swedish parliament. Then just 15 years old, she had decided to skip lessons to demand urgent action on the climate crisis. She declared in early September that she would repeat the strike every Friday until Sweden aligned with the Paris Agreement, which was by then nearly three years old. The idea caught the imagination of young people around the world, many of whom had been searching for an outlet for their fear and frustration about the gloomy predictions of the impacts of climate change. In February 2019, an estimated 15,000 students and children stayed away from the classroom and gathered on the streets of major cities across the United Kingdom. The protestors vowed to strike from school once a month on a Friday until serious action was undertaken. Youth Strike for Climate activists announced that the biggest strike yet would be held on Friday 15 March 2019, with a major demonstration planned for London.

The second of these movements was Extinction Rebellion (XR) which emerged in autumn 2018 led by a group of academics and activists including Roger Hallam and Gail Bradbrook. Though picked up by the media, the first few actions by the group did not immediately spark the widespread interest which was to come. Around a thousand people turned out for a Declaration of Rebellion in Parliament Square on 31 October 2018. The group included activists who had been involved in previous disruptive protest movements or non-violent direct action, such as Stop Killing Londoners (members jumped in front of London buses or laid down in the road to protest at air pollution) and the Occupy movement (which had camped out on the steps of St Paul's Cathedral for several months in 2011). XR adopted tactics including street theatre, wearing masks, supergluing people to buildings and important sites, obstruction and blocking roads. Frustrated by the perceived lack of action by politicians to implement reforms of the scale necessary to avert climate breakdown, a hard core of the activists decided in those early months that they were willing to risk arrest and possible charges in order to draw attention to the problem. Many of these tactics and strategies had been tried before by environmental campaigners including Greenpeace and Plane Stupid, but had had a limited impact on the public consciousness. Something in the *zeitgeist* of late 2018 meant that XR seemed to be pushing at an open door.

In a foreshadowing of what was to come, one Saturday afternoon in November 2018 about 5,000 people gathered on five London bridges. Although many of them were moved on by the police, they quickly regrouped using social media and What's App to coordinate, and succeeded in blocking Westminster Bridge completely for several hours. The atmosphere was calm, and many families with small children and elderly people mingled happily in the frosty air with the more predictable white dreadlocked activists.[25] Over the next few months, Extinction Rebellion went on to shock and inspire through tactics such as pouring buckets of red paint onto the pavement outside Downing Street, lying down in front of the traffic on the busy Elephant and Castle roundabout in London and taking off their clothes and gluing themselves to the glass of the viewing gallery in the House of Commons.

The second international youth climate strike took place on 12 April 2019. This time tens of thousands of young people missed school and went out onto the streets. At Parliament Square, the young people quickly overwhelmed police barriers. They hung from trees and boarded several red buses that had got caught at the traffic lights at the end of Westminster Bridge. Traffic built up all around the Square and a long queue of black cabs, some with their engines idling, built up along Victoria Street. The grass square opposite Parliament rapidly became a soggy mud pit. The atmosphere was electric, with impassioned young people cheering and singing, waving placards and hugging. Under the calm gaze of Millicent Fawcett, a group of mothers with tiny babies and pushchairs laid out picnic blankets, many of them breastfeeding, sharing food, with toddlers playing in the mud.

Three days later XR launched its first international rebellion. This was a week that saw the group's profile explode from a fringe interest for seasoned environmentalists to something that almost everyone was talking about. In London, the group launched simultaneous protests at Waterloo, Parliament Square, Marble Arch and Oxford Circus. The speed and flexibility of the protestors took police by surprise, and within hours Waterloo Bridge was closed to traffic and huge tailbacks had formed three miles away on Park Lane. Oxford Circus fell silent, and activists unveiled a giant pink boat named *Berta* after the murdered Honduran indigenous activist Berta Cáceres. By the next day Waterloo Bridge had been transformed into something approaching a mini-festival. Protestors constructed gazebos from which they handed out food, sun cream and advice to the occupiers who were sleeping in tents on the tarmac. A few people played drums and guitars, people arrived carrying flowers and pot plants, cakes, ribbons, flags and cushions. That day the police began to arrest protestors who refused to move when approached, but they had to stop when they ran out of holding cells in the capital. At Hyde Park, passers-by commented on how they could suddenly hear bird song without the constant roar of traffic. Haulage firms and bus drivers complained as the traffic backed up and drivers searched frantically for alternative points to cross the River Thames. For a few days, the speed and scale of the tactics meant the protestors had the upper hand. The Metropolitan Police seemed reluctant to intervene forcefully, and some of those offering themselves up for arrest were elderly people, middle-class, educated and non-violent. By the end of the week nearly 700 people had been arrested, cells across London were full of activists and hundreds of supporters had turned up to provide food and legal observer services.

In the weeks that followed the climate crisis hit the front pages. On 18 April, the BBC aired an hour-long documentary, 'Climate change: the facts' presented by national treasure David Attenborough. Attenborough's career showcasing the best of the natural world had for many years evaded the issue of humanity's impact upon it. He had been criticised by many such as George Monbiot for not using his position to raise awareness of the destruction wreaked by humans. 'Blue chip' natural history programmes had continued to appear regardless, allegedly sometimes filmed from angles that disguised human impact on habitats that were made to look pristine and undisturbed. Climate change was considered negative and depressing and editors feared it would lose them viewers. But beginning with his hard-hitting Netflix series 'Our Planet', Attenborough's position changed. His new series described climate change as humanity's 'greatest threat in thousands of years' and showed harrowing scenes of wildfires and mass deaths of heat-exhausted flying foxes. Attenborough did not shy away from blaming fossil fuel companies for sowing uncertainty about the science as a way to secure obscene profits over many years. The programmes were sobering and distressing to watch.

At the other end of the generational scale, Greta Thunberg moved from obscure teenage activist to household name. On 24 April she was invited to speak at an event in Westminster hosted by the Green MP Caroline Lucas. The UK environment secretary Michael Gove was there and told her afterwards 'Your voice has been heard'. The next week Labour leader Jeremy Corbyn tabled a motion in Parliament to declare a national climate emergency and commit the UK to achieving Net Zero emissions by 2050. The motion was responding to one of the key demands of XR, and followed several declarations of emergency by local authorities across the country.

Twelve years – the case for urgency

Another significant event that added to the public's growing realisation that the climate crisis was already here was the publication of a seminal report by the Intergovernmental Panel on Climate Change in October 2018, although governments had been given advance warning of what it contained earlier in the year. The IPCC report has been called the 'twelve-year report'.

The headline achievement of the Paris Agreement was a commitment by signatory countries to try to limit global temperature rises to 'well below' 2°C above pre-industrial averages, and to pursue 'efforts to limit the temperature increase to 1.5°C'. Paris was the first international treaty to give the 2°C limit legal effect, but as we have seen there had been a battle between the High Ambition Coalition and some oil-producing states at the

2015 CoP over whether the 1.5°C limit should be included. This betokened a deep unease between those who understood the science and those who understood the need for a politically acceptable deal to which countries could sign up, which remains today. As part of the follow-on from the Paris Agreement, the IPCC was charged with producing a synthesis of the best available scientific evidence to highlight the different consequences of the warming scenarios of 1.5°C and 2°C. In October 2018, the true inadequacy of the 2°C limit became common knowledge. In 'Global warming of 1.5°C' the IPCC synthesised more than 6,000 scientific references. The conclusion was stark: 'climate models project robust differences in regional climate characteristics between present-day and global warming of 1.5°C, and between 1.5°C and 2°C',[26] that included higher land and sea temperatures, increased precipitation, floods, droughts, extreme weather events and more frequent (and hotter) extreme high temperatures. If average temperature rises could be limited to 1.5°C, by 2100 the sea would rise 10cm less than under a 2°C scenario, affecting 10 million fewer people. It was anticipated that 18% of insect species would lose over half of their climatically determined geographic range under a 2°C scenario, but 'only' 6% under a 1.5°C limit. Similar threats were uttered for food and water supply, the future of coral reefs (almost all of which would be lost with a 2°C rise) and sea ice, increases in ocean acidification and melting permafrost.

Whereas ten years previously scientists had at times lost themselves in worthy attempts to explain that all predictions come with uncertainty, by 2018 no-one was mincing words. The IPCC report concluded that without dramatic cuts to emissions in the immediate future, the opportunity to stop the warming rising above 1.5°C would be lost by 2030. Written in 2018, this was summarised as 'twelve years left to act'. Crucially, the scientists concluded that Net Zero globally needed to be achieved by 2050 in order to have a chance of meeting the 1.5°C limit, and that by 2030 we needed to be well on the path to significantly reducing emissions.

The IPCC report became a clarion call for environmental activism. Its publication dovetailed with the establishment of the Youth Strike for Climate and Extinction Rebellion protest movements in late 2018 and early 2019. Something about the twelve-year time frame and the clarity of the scientific message seemed to resonate. The urgency of this deadline seeped into a wider public consciousness giving these movements extra impact. These ground-shifting developments in public understanding and clamour for action took place at exactly the same time as the Heathrow JR was being prepared. The world was waking up to the dangers of climate change and the need for urgency. Could the courts be relied on to understand why it was so important for the UK to embrace the implications of the Paris Agreement and the race to Net Zero?

The High Court case fails

Wednesday 1 May 2019 was a funny day for climate action. In the morning, at the Printworks everyone was on tenterhooks as the legal team waited for the High Court judgment. FoE was busy planning to orient a significant part of its campaigning towards harnessing this wave of awareness and concern about climate breakdown. Many staff had been working hard to add support to the demonstrations led by Youth Strike for Climate, and a new campaign was being designed around Donald Trump's planned visit to London in June 2019. In the treehouse area, about twenty papier maché 'Earth-heads' with sad faces sat on a table and looked on as the staff waited for the call. XR protests were continuing, with more than 1,000 people arrested. Many staff genuinely thought a corner had been turned, and dared to hope that climate breakdown might yet be averted.

But it was not to be for the Heathrow case. Just after 10am the politics team took the call from Will Rundle at the court. The JR had failed on all counts. The office fell quiet. How could it be that the court did not share the view that building a new runway during a climate emergency would throw all the UK's climate commitments into question? It seemed not to make sense. A few minutes after the call, Craig Bennett marched into the main office, heading straight for the press team. Bennett is a tall, imposing man with dark eyebrows that give him a permanent look of determination. People peeped over at him from behind their screens, watching as he gesticulated wildly; the press team scribbled notes as he prepared a quote on the fly. After a few minutes of hushed discussion, he banged the desk with his fist and declared 'We'll appeal! That's it. Let's prepare an appeal!' Claire from the press team rubbed her hands nervously through her short brown hair before picking up the phone to the broadsheets as Bennett marched back to his office.

But that was not the end of the drama that day. Later that afternoon, the XR protestors got what they wanted. Just two miles to the north of the FoE offices, large crowds were still gathered at Parliament Square. Some had tied themselves with ropes into the mature London plane trees which circle the little strip of grass in the middle of a noisy roundabout, which after weeks of demonstrations looked more like a Glastonbury field than central London. Police tape flapped at the edge of cordons wound across the pedestrian crossing in front of Westminster, where groups of young people sat around in the sunshine with bedraggled placards. Inside the Palace of Westminster, MPs were debating a Labour party proposal to pass a climate emergency motion.

After what seemed like hours, Labour leader Jeremy Corbyn emerged from the chamber and, climbing on a fire engine that was parked in Parliament Square, he addressed the crowd with a loudhailer. Parliament had voted in favour of declaring an emergency and Corbyn called on the government to put in place plans to achieve Net Zero greenhouse gas emissions by 2050. Although the vote did not compel the government to act, it had been a key demand of protestors. An enormous cheer went up from the crowd. Would this mean that politicians might finally put their money where their mouths were?

'There was a deep sense of irony that the court found that the in-principle policy support for Heathrow was legal on the same day that Parliament declared this emergency,' Katie de Kauwe told me later.[27]

So why had the JR failed? To briefly summarise, the substance of the Hillingdon claimants' argument surrounded traffic management and predictions of the impact an extra 240,000 flights a year would have on the number of vehicles travelling to the airport and on associated air pollution targets. A second strand of their argument rested on the EU Habitats Directive and they argued that the Airports Commission had been wrong to exclude Gatwick as an alternative. The Hillingdon claimants argued that Gatwick should still be considered if it had the potential to offer better protection. Another point had centred on the quality and conclusions of the appraisal of sustainability

(AoS) which was carried out as part of the ANPS, and which effectively acted as the required SEA; they argued that indicative flight paths were insufficient to predict how many extra people would be affected by overflying and aircraft noise if the third runway went ahead, and that the precautionary principle required more accurate modelling.

The High Court decided that Grayling had acted properly in his assessment of the traffic estimates, and that adequate mitigation measures had been put in place.[28] The thrust of these conclusions was that the ANPS was sufficiently robust and that detailed plans to reduce the number of private car journeys and other issues would be offered in the DCO application. On air quality, the High Court was unconvinced by the claimants' concerns that uncertainty over the impacts on air quality and the effectiveness of mitigation measures risked breaching the precautionary principle. The judgment fell back on the argument that if at the DCO stage the Secretary of State was unconvinced that the runway plans would sufficiently mitigate the risk of further deterioration in air quality, consent would be withheld. Teddington Action Group's arguments on air quality and the effects of air pollution from aircraft themselves were also rejected by the court, as were the claims from the team representing Jock Lowe and the rival runway extension scheme.

The High Court rejected all of the crucial climate arguments. The court noted that, as the UK has a dualist legal system, any international treaty the country signs (e.g. the Paris Agreement) will have no domestic legal force until it has been implemented by a national statute. The 1.5°C temperature limit had yet to be incorporated into UK legislation because, in 2016, the CCC had advised that the CCA 08 target did not yet need to change. The court ruled that neither international treaty nor policy can override domestic statute (in this case CCA 08), and therefore concluded that the Secretary of State had been correct to rely on that domestic law and not the international treaty. It also observed that the Paris Agreement does not place any legally binding commitment on countries to achieve carbon reductions. It merely requires them to outline their contributions in an NDC, and to commit to trying to achieve these reductions. Thirdly, the court found that it could not be accepted that the government had clearly rejected the 80% reduction target by 2018, no matter how much the campaigners argued that the government must have been aware of the implications of the IPCC report. The court found that the target of the CCA 08 was firmly entrenched government policy at the time the ANPS was designated in 2018, rejecting Plan B's section 5 policy argument. It reiterated that government policy is based on statute, something Friends of the Earth had accepted during the hearing.

The court was at pains to explain that all this did not necessarily mean that the 80% reduction target and the 2°C temperature limit were *correct*. It merely established that these were government policy at the time of the decision and that therefore the Secretary of State had been entitled to rely on those targets in coming to his decision. This judgment applied to all aspects of the claims, including the SEA.

Again, the court rejected FoE's much broader section 10 argument. It judged that, although Grayling had acknowledged that he had not taken Paris into account, merely relying on the CCA 2008, he was within his rights to have used his discretion to decide that. The Planning Act 2008 and the CCA 2008 had been passed on the same day and court held that it was clear that their climate change aspects were meant to be read together, and at the time of the judgment relying on the 80% reduction target would meet the requirement to ensure sustainable development. The court disagreed that section 10 required the Secretary of State to bear in mind broader factors such as the impacts of post-2050 warming and non-CO_2 warming.

There was, however, better news in the judgment about FoE's attempts to get more clarity about what the ANPS actually means. David Wolfe had argued in the initial hearing that it was unclear how the phrase 'material impact on the ability of the Government to meet its carbon reduction targets' would be interpreted in terms of assessing the runway scheme's impact on the UK's overall emissions, in particular emissions from planes in flight. The team also argued that it was not clear from the ANPS whether any DCO application would be assessed against the emissions reductions targets as they stood in 2018 – an 80% reduction – or as they stood at the time of the application. Given that the campaigners felt sure that a commitment to Net Zero would have to come at some point in the future, would the third runway be assessed against that new target?

The judges did not agree that the ANPS was insufficiently clear. They found that policy statements could be expected to leave certain matters to be interpreted in more detail by decision makers at the DCO stage, and that the ANPS contained an adequate level of guidance. 'The assessment of the impact of carbon emissions at the stage of development consent will clearly include emissions from aircraft using Heathrow in flight. There is nothing in paragraph 5.82 to exclude such emissions. Again, Mr Maurici submitted that the ANPS was unambiguously clear in this respect. We agree.'[29] In other words, any developer would struggle to argue in court a reading of the ANPS which suggested that an airport is only responsible for the emissions from construction, the airport buildings and ground operations, and *not* from the actual planes using it. The court also found that the carbon reduction targets were effectively not 'frozen' in time. This confirmed for all future DCO applications that any proposed development would be assessed against climate commitments *as they stand when the DCO application is made.*

Although FoE lost this point, barrister Pete Lockley explains that this was essentially a tactic used by the campaigners to get clarification of the meaning of the ANPS, which could be of use later. Since today the UK has accepted the commitment to meet Net Zero emissions by 2050, it looks as though it will be substantially harder to show that a new runway does not jeopardise this.

These two points are very important clarifications to have secured, and may become key to any future legal challenges if Heathrow Airport is granted a DCO by the government.

CCC recommends Net Zero

Concluding that the government had not erred by considering the impacts of airport expansion with reference to the CCA 08 and its targets was one thing while the government's independent climate change advisors were still recommending that this target did not need to change. This was officially the case on 1 May 2019, the day of the High Court judgment.

But the next day, 2 May 2019, was another funny old day in climate action. In another spectacular irony, the day after the High Court ruled in the Heathrow JR that the 80% reduction/2°C targets had indeed been the correct basis for the assessments justifying the ANPS, the CCC published a new report which for the first time called on the government to amend that CCA 08 target. The report was the CCC's response to the calls for Net Zero – themselves a response to the Paris Agreement, and clearly referenced the steeper emissions cuts necessary to seek to limit temperature rises to 1.5°C. The day after the High Court effectively ruled that it had been unnecessary to consider Paris when drawing up airport expansion plans, the CCC now recommended that the temperature basis for the ANPS was obsolete. 'We conclude that net-zero is necessary, feasible and cost-effective. Necessary – to respond to the overwhelming evidence of the role of greenhouse gases in driving global climate change, and to meet the UK's commitments as a signatory of the 2015 Paris Agreement.'[30]

The CCC's updated advice paved the way for Parliament to vote in June 2019 in favour of amending the target of the CCA 2008 from an 80% reduction to achieving Net Zero by 2050. This vote in favour of increasing ambition followed months of intense climate campaigning by Fridays for Future and Extinction Rebellion, in tandem with a notable increase in media coverage.

Including emissions from aviation and shipping

And there was more news about emissions from aviation and shipping in the CCC's new report.

Just to recap, CCA 08 did not require emissions from IAS to be formally included in carbon budgets and the CCC had maintained that international aviation emissions were best dealt with at the international level, reflecting those international efforts with a somewhat arcane 'headroom' system in the UK's carbon budgets. We saw the planning assumption that emissions from aviation would not exceed 37.5MtCO2e a year by 2050, and that this would allow other sectors to plan the scale of their emissions reductions, either through emissions trading or through an emissions cap through demand management, tax and regulation. In either case, aviation's status as a hard-to-treat sector meant that other industries would have to work harder, decarbonising by 85% to allow aviation to continue to pollute. The CCC had previously seemed unwilling to openly call for a change in this position.

However, in their new report, the CCC finally took a tougher line on aviation: 'emissions from international aviation and shipping cannot be ignored' it stated.[31] The differences in responsibility between other industries and aviation were glaring, with the Committee noting that they expected the aviation sector to emit more GHGs than any other sector (up from 2.5% of current emissions), possibly up to a quarter of the carbon budget by 2050.

Recommending that aviation must start pulling its weight in this new Net Zero world was significant. David Joffe, head of carbon budgets at the CCC, explains that the new target meant there was less 'wiggle room' in terms of which sectors could avoid rapid decarbonisation. As we have seen, the UK's carbon budgets present the total amount of carbon that may be emitted, and this allowance is carved up between sectors. An 80% reduction world suggested that 20% of the economy could feasibly avoid having to decarbonise; 'Under the old 80% emissions reduction target, many sectors assumed they didn't need to do much. Way more than 20% of emitters were "hiding" in the last 20%,' says Joffe. 'With Net Zero, it is clearer – you need to reduce emissions as close to zero as possible.'[32] While the CCC tries to suggest approaches by modelling different scenarios to give politicians a choice of which difficult decisions to take, and which to avoid, ultimately under Net Zero everyone has to pull their weight sooner or later.

The CCC Net Zero report modelled a number of possible scenarios covering how aviation could meet its obligations if IAS were included in the next round of carbon budgeting. The CCC was unenthusiastic about the use of offsetting while simultaneously allowing unrestricted growth in passenger numbers. The aviation modelling assumed that aviation fuel might become more sustainable, and technical efficiency savings such as airspace modernisation might contribute, *to a degree*. It still allowed for demand for flying to increase by 60% over 2005 levels, but this was significantly below the DfT's projections which saw demand for flights increasing by 90% by 2050. Therefore, for the first time ever, the CCC introduced the concept-that-dare-not-speak-its-name in the aviation world – demand management:

> without additional policies being put in place, government projections suggest demand could be higher than this [90% ...] New UK policies will therefore be needed to manage growth in demand. These could include carbon pricing, reforms to Air Passenger Duty, or policies to manage the use of airport capacity.[33]

It is worth clarifying that this was a recommendation, not to reduce current demand, but only to implement policies to restrict *growth in demand*.

When the government legislated the Net Zero target in June 2019, the CCC's advice to include IAS emissions was not initially heeded. However, the government signalled that Net Zero should cover the whole economy and committed to writing to the CCC to ask for advice on how to achieve this. In September 2019, Lord Deben wrote formally to the new transport secretary Grant Shapps, outlining the steps that the government must take to bring emissions from IAS within the UK's target to reach Net Zero emissions by 2050. His letter again warned that failing to include IAS in the target would mean more ambitious targets in other sectors would probably be required in the future. It argued that the primary policy approach to reducing IAS emissions should be at the international level through schemes such as CORSIA and EU ETS, given the global nature of these sectors and the risk of carbon leakage from a unilateral UK approach; however, domestic policies would still have an important role. Finally, the letter recommended that emissions could be reduced even further 'by limiting demand growth to at most 25% above current levels (2018)'.[34] And in what seemed like a killer blow to Heathrow expansion plans, the CCC spoke out against expanding airport capacity in the UK. The advisors recommended that the government 'should assess its airport capacity strategy in this context'. Specifically, it warned that increasing capacity in London, and at Heathrow, would leave 'at most, very limited room for growth at non-London airports'.

The appeal

When the appeal hearing came round in late October 2019, things had moved on again. 'You never know where a case will end up; it never ends where it started. By the time of the Court of Appeal's judgment, the context had changed, we now had Net Zero. That was encouraging for the wider context to the case,' says Rowan Smith from Leigh Day.[35] But even as the teams from Plan B and FoE prepared their cases, the fever pitch of climate action seemed to die away again. An incident at Canning Town underground station in October saw an XR protestor dragged off the roof of a tube train while angry passengers shouted at him for disrupting their morning commute. XR organisers admitted the act was a mistake. Another XR uprising for November 2019 hit the headlines, but saw fewer protestors than the previous movement.

In moving forward to appeal, two of the original claimants – the Hillingdon group and rival runway bid teams – decided against running another challenge. Plan B and FoE were now free to advance and defend their original climate arguments, so they appealed against the whole judgment. Only FoE's section 5 grounds (the clarity of the ANPS wording) were not brought forward, as the team were happy that the High Court verdict had sufficiently established what the DCO application would consider – that the process *would* consider the impacts of emissions from planes in flight and that the climate targets would not be frozen in time. The team felt it had been sufficiently established that a developer submitting a DCO application would need to show the expansion plans would not jeopardise the Net Zero target, not the old 80% target.

The lawyers' preparations focused on trying to draw the judge's attention to the 'obviously material' aspect of the Planning Act language, which in legalese means that by law the government is required to take something into account. The teams knew that the court decision would focus only on whether the decision had been made following legally correct procedures, so it was paramount to establish the importance of considering the Paris Agreement to an infrastructure project on the scale of the third runway.

During the appeal court hearing, Tim Crosland felt that the mood was different to that in the High Court. This time the case was heard by Lord Justice Lindblom, Senior President of Tribunals, who has a strong background in planning cases. He was joined by Lord Justice Singh who has written extensively about human rights and Lord Justice Haddon-Cave who has a background in aviation law. Crosland felt that this time the judges focused more on trying to understand what was inside the enormous bundles of court documents, particularly the scientific reports about non-CO_2 warming and the IPCC report.

> I felt that one of the judges, Rabinder Singh, got the point that the government had told the public Heathrow expansion was consistent with its international obligations on climate change, when it knew that to be untrue. The High Court just didn't want to know about that – or the difference between 1.5°C and 2°C warming. This time the Court seemed to pick up the scent that something had gone badly wrong: the public and Parliament had been dangerously misled. We always believed that as long as the court had the courage to look the facts in the face, everything else could fall into place.[36]

Friends of the Earth's Katie de Kauwe also felt that there was more of a challenge during these hearings: 'It's always really difficult to tell what a court is thinking,' she says. 'But there was certainly a feeling that our case was being well presented, and that the judges were engaged in what we were saying, which gave us real hope.'[37]

The legal teams had to wait another four months for the judgment. As 2020 began, a little virus was busy making its way all around the world without anyone much noticing. The first case of coronavirus had been reported in the UK at the end of January. Even on 27 February, when the judgment in the appeal was announced just a week before the first death in the UK from coronavirus occurred, no-one paid much attention to the gathering storm. Teams from all sides crammed into the courtroom at the Royal Courts of Justice on the Strand, and supporters gathered in a crowd outside the building. FoE's key legal team already knew the result. They had been sitting on the most exciting news for four days, unable to break the court's embargo, even to their colleagues. On the Monday before the public announcement, Will Rundle had received the message of a lifetime. Friends of the Earth and Plan B had won their climate cases. A draft copy of the judgment was sent around to the claimants; the Court of Appeal had overturned the High Court's rejection of all the grounds.

'It was so hard keeping quiet about this' says Craig Bennett. 'We aren't allowed to tell anyone, so for four days before the news was made public the three of us had to walk around the office with this incredible secret, pretending all the while that we weren't sure how it was going to go. It was surreal.'[38]

When it was announced on 27 February 2020 the judgment was a bombshell. Climate campaigners everywhere celebrated, with many legal analysts quickly suggesting that this could be the beginning of a string of cases invoking the utmost importance of the Paris Agreement. It seemed a decisive moment in giving the Paris Agreement on Climate Change some tangibility in domestic law. 'Its implications are global,' said Margaretha Wewerinke-Singh, an international public law expert at Leiden University. 'For the first time, a court has confirmed that the Paris Agreement temperature goal has binding effect. This goal was based on overwhelming evidence about the catastrophic risk of exceeding 1.5C of warming. Yet some have argued that the goal is aspirational only, leaving governments free to ignore it in practice.'[39] The lawyers were rightly proud of themselves. Will Rundle was named 'Lawyer of the Week' in *The Times* for his role in the challenge. Later that week the FoE legal team headed to a pub in Holborn near the Royal Courts of Justice. The celebration coincided with Craig Bennett's leaving party; he had just been appointed CEO of the Wildlife Trusts. The team, and in fact just about everyone else, were unaware that this would be one of the last big nights out for a while.

The Court of Appeal judgment looked at the same evidence on the applicability of the Paris Agreement that the High Court had examined, and came to a substantially different conclusion. Whereas the High Court had concluded that Grayling was correct to have discounted Paris as 'not relevant' since it was an unincorporated treaty, relying instead on the UK's statutory 80% reduction target in CCA 08, the Court of Appeal disagreed. Relying on a judgment by Lord Brown of Eaton-under-Heywood in *Hurst*, at paragraphs 57 to 59, the court recalled 'that there are some international treaties that are so *obviously material* (my emphasis) that they must be considered'. As far as the Court of Appeal was concerned these included the Paris Agreement.

There was more to come. On FoE's section 10 Planning Act broader duty on climate and sustainability ground, that the minister was obliged to consider international treaties in ensuring that the ANPS contributed to mitigating climate change, the court was unequivocal:

> If he had asked himself that question, and insofar as he did, the only answer that would reasonably have been open to him is that the Paris Agreement was so obviously material to the decision he

had to make in deciding whether to designate the ANPS that it was irrational not to take it into account.[40]

This was an extraordinary outcome, as irrationality is considered the highest threshold for a JR to meet. Only a handful of JRs are won on this ground, according to the Institute of Government.[41]

The Court of Appeal went on. Noting that the CCC's 2016 advice that an 80% reduction requirement could be 'potentially consistent' with Paris's aspirational 1.5°C limit, the court found that this did not irrefutably prove that it was. On the SEA ground, again the court found that it was quite clear that objectives agreed at the international level need to be taken into consideration when assessing a project for climate impacts. The Court of Appeal found that the lower court had failed to provide reasoning why the section 10 grounds should fail. And there was more drama to come. The court found that, while there was continuing scientific uncertainty as to the durability of the non-CO2 warming effects of aviation – how long NO_2, soot particles and water vapour stay in the atmosphere – there was much less disagreement about the impact of those emissions. We have seen that the scientific consensus is that the impact is in the region of thrice the warming potential of CO2 alone. The court found in favour of Katie de Kauwe's argument:

> In line with the precautionary principle, and as common sense might suggest, scientific uncertainty is not a reason for not taking something into account at all, even if it cannot be precisely quantified at that stage.[42]

This was an incredible outcome for Katie, so soon in her career at Friends of the Earth and the first time she'd been involved in a case of this magnitude. 'When I read the draft judgment, I was thrilled to see the Court of Appeal had accepted my idea,' she told me.[43]

Turning to Plan B's argument, the court found for the argument that by 2018 government policy was firmly behind alignment with Paris. The judgment was simple. Whereas the lower court had argued that the term 'government policy' could only be based on the requirements of statute – in this case, CCA 08 – the Court of Appeal ruled that 'government policy' does not have a special meaning in English. Therefore, there was no reason to limit 'policy' to meaning only what legislation stated. Ministers had referred to Paris alignment as early as 2016, and Parliament had ratified the Paris agreement. The court judged that this was sufficient for it to be considered as policy. Furthermore, the court found that CCA 08 actually requires '*at least*' an 80% reduction (my emphasis), which was not inconsistent with strengthening ambition in line with the Paris 1.5°C limit.

The Court of Appeal effectively declared the ANPS a void policy. The designation was declared unlawful, and the court ordered the Secretary of State to undertake a review in light of its conclusions. Another delay to the third runway project had been secured. Significantly, the government announced that it would not appeal the judgment.

This section of the judgment reflects the significance of the victory:

The legal issues are of the highest importance. The infrastructure project under consideration is one of the largest. Both the development itself and its effects will last well into the second half of this century. The issue of climate change is a matter of profound national and international importance and of great concern to the public – and indeed, to the government of the United Kingdom and many other national governments, as is demonstrated by their commitment to the Paris Agreement.[44]

FoE argued that the judgment had other far-reaching impacts. In a post-judgment briefing, Will Rundle argued that it meant that when all the existing NPSs on energy, transport, ports, etc. are reviewed from time to time, the Paris Agreement must be taken into account. These documents would need to show that the application of Paris could be explained in order to contribute to 'sustainable development' with particular regard to mitigating climate change. Rundle argued that any new infrastructure NPSs must also be drawn up according to the same principles. The duty to consider the warming impacts beyond 2050 and the non-CO2 warming impacts had also been established.[45]

Taking account of the Paris Agreement

The Paris Agreement had been central to the appeals court judgment. The court clearly found that transport secretary Chris Grayling had erred in judgement by not taking the international agreement into consideration on multiple occasions while making his decision about whether to accept the draft ANPS. The Paris Agreement requires efforts to stabilise temperatures at 1.5°C above pre-industrial times, recognising that 2°C will not be enough. But by his own admission – and those in the DfT witness statements revealed at the pre-trial hearing – Grayling had assessed the north-west runway scheme against 2°C. It was clear in the text of the ANPS that the CCA 08 80% reduction target had been the only target taken into account in the official assessment. The ANPS made no mention of the Paris Agreement. It had been established that the Secretary of

State had misunderstood the nature of the broader duty on him under section 10 Planning Act to take into consideration the wider policy and international context. The court had established that Paris was 'obviously material' to any consideration of the climate impacts of new infrastructure projects. This was the substance of the victory.

The judgment and the reams of documentation and legal arguments that surrounded it threw up a number of difficult points. They exposed the policy of not including GHG emissions from IAS in any national targets. They also showed that aviation had been a glaring omission from the Paris Agreement. The can had been kicked down the road to continue the system of trying to regulate aviation emissions under the auspices of ICAO, but ICAO's CORSIA scheme only aimed for carbon-neutral *growth* from a 2020 baseline. The 2020 Court of Appeal judgment threw unwelcome light on the inherent contradiction in a global community, and the UK with it, trying to meet the emissions reduction requirements of the Paris Agreement without dealing with an aviation sector which was fast becoming one of the biggest polluters. It seemed to many that the aviation industry was getting a free pass to pollute while other sectors such as road transport, home heating and power generation were being expected to make ground-breaking, rapid changes to bring down emissions. By excluding aviation, Paris had not gone far enough.

The government did not dispute the Court of Appeal's judgment, and did not seek to appeal it. The JR outcome would now require them to reassess the decision to designate the ANPS, and to use the Paris Agreement as a point of reference. However, there was no guarantee a reconsidered decision would be any different.

Heathrow was not going to wait about while the reassessment took place. Within weeks it signalled its intention to appeal (as a party interested in the case it had the right), adding that the climate concerns that the Court of Appeal had highlighted were 'eminently fixable'. They were not the only ones to disagree with the judgment. There were certainly a number of raised eyebrows in the legal community. Overturning every ground in a High Court judgment was greeted with surprise by some in a traditionally conservative world. The government's barrister James Maurici, speaking in 2021, says that the judgment was called 'brave' in some quarters, which he explains can be a polite way of saying 'wrong'. The *Law Quarterly Review* called it a 'flight of fancy'.[46]

Tim Crosland and all the Friends of the Earth legal team were not going to let that spoil their day. 'It was such a clear and well-reasoned judgment,' says Crosland. 'It felt like a truth had been spoken – the Paris Agreement limit, on which the habitability of the planet depends, had legal significance and the bell was tolling on the carbon economy. We really felt like it could never be put back in the box.'[47]

Supreme Court case

The euphoria did not last. Days after the Court of Appeal judgment was announced, the UK went into lockdown following the explosion in coronavirus cases. The effects on the airline industry and demand for flights were immediate. Early on in the pandemic, John Hollande-Kaye said that the collapse in demand meant that the new runway might not be needed for another ten years (we will return to this in Chapter 4). But even with this crisis in its core business, Heathrow Airport ploughed on. On 6 May 2020, the company was given permission to appeal to the Supreme Court.

Meanwhile, the government seemed to quietly shelve its support of the north-west runway project. Grant Shapps, the new transport minister, signalled that the government would abide by the Court of Appeal's judgment and not contest it at the higher court. He reiterated that any expansion of the airport would be industry-led, and that the government took its environmental commitments seriously.[48] The only other remaining pro-expansion claimant, Arora Group, decided against joining the Supreme Court appeal in the light of the negative economic impact on the aviation industry caused by the pandemic.

The Supreme Court is the final court charged with adjudicating the most pressing cases of national interest. It was established after the Constitutional Reform Act of 2005 which sought to clarify the separation of powers in the UK by moving the Law Lords (lords with judicial functions) out of the House of Lords and into the Middlesex Guildhall across the road. It heard its first case in 2009, and since then 'arguably its most important case' was to rule that prime minister Boris Johnson had broken the law by proroguing Parliament in 2019.[49] The Heathrow case was heard in October 2020, with five judges (there is always an odd number of judges so a decision can be by majority). The bench included the Scottish judge Lord Reed, perhaps best known for his dissenting judgment in the controversial Brexit case which ordered the government to consult Parliament before triggering Article 50 to begin the process of leaving the European Union; Deputy President Lord Hodge, Deputy President Lady Black, Lord Leggatt and Lord Sales, one of the judges branded an 'enemy of the people' by the *Daily Mail* following the Article 50 decision.

In contrast to the showy demonstrations and news cameras outside the appeals court just seven months previously, the case was heard entirely online. It was another huge hearing with hours of complex testimony delivered over two days of video conferencing, which was a challenge for all parties. 'It was surreal over Zoom,' says Tim Crosland. 'The dynamics were very different to an ordinary court hearing; for example, the judges had to use the "hand up" function if they wanted to say something.'[50]

Heathrow Airport was represented by Lord Anderson QC, the government's former independent reviewer of terrorism legislation, who has argued a number of significant cases on free speech. He spoke eloquently of the UK's history as a climate leader, referencing the significance of CCA 08 having been the world's first legislation to set legally binding emissions reduction targets. This formed the basis of his argument, which aimed to persuade the judges that with such a solid piece of legislation against which to evaluate potential infrastructure projects, it was unnecessary to rely on the Paris Agreement as an unincorporated treaty. He spoke of technological advances in aviation which were being developed, such as sustainable aviation fuel and carbon offsets, which would mean, he argued, that the third runway plans could be developed within the UK's allotted carbon budgets set out in CCA 08. He raised the scientific uncertainty around the issue of the durability of the non-CO_2 warming impacts of aviation. Part of Lord Anderson's speech referenced the *old* 80% emissions reduction target, because this was the law as it had stood when the ANPS was designated in 2018. It was somewhat surreal to listen to this, given that everyone knew this target was now discredited and more than eighteen months had passed since the government had committed to Net Zero. It was even more surreal to consider that this was a private company arguing that the government had considered the Paris Agreement, when ten months previously the same government had effectively conceded that it had not and had accepted the ruling of the Court of Appeal.

There were a couple of technical hiccups with the video link during the hearing, and for legal professionals who are used to addressing a court room it must have been hard to speak convincingly into a tiny webcam. Crosland was arguing against a polished exposition of the UK's climate leadership from Lord Anderson. 'Even judges are susceptible to fairy tales,' he told me later. 'They want to be told that it's all OK, that nothing has to really change. They want to believe that the UK is leading the way, and that the problem is everyone else.'[51]

For the next two months, the campaigners waited for the judgment. This was not the only anxious wait for Will Rundle – he was expecting his first child. A little girl was born on 15 December, the day before the judgment was announced. As Will tried to tie up loose ends before his new arrival, while facing the threat of yet another winter coronavirus lockdown, he remained outwardly confident that at least one of the grounds might stick. In particular, he thought the non-CO2 warming impacts could be a crucial factor pushing the verdict the way of the campaigners.[52] The campaigners kept a brave face on, but it was clear in my conversations with several of them that they knew the risks were high.

CCC launches the UK's sixth carbon budget

As all parties waited for the Supreme Court verdict, presumably Heathrow Airport was hoping that a positive outcome would finally draw a line under the arguments for and against a third runway. However, the thorny issue of whether to formally include IAS emissions in the UK's carbon budgets had still not been resolved. And this legal case was developing a funny tendency for judgments to arrive at the same time as significant changes in climate policy. These confluences have only served to draw attention to the inconsistencies.

On 9 December 2020, just a week before the Supreme Court handed down its judgment, the CCC issued its sixth carbon budget recommendations, covering targets for the UK to meet between 2033 and 2037. The document represented a significant ratcheting-up of climate ambition. Although it was acknowledged that good progress had been made in decarbonising energy production, the CCC's overall message was austere. In line with the Net Zero commitment, the proposed budget required an overall 78% reduction in GHG emissions from 1990 levels by 2035, effectively achieving emissions cuts in half the period that had been allowed in the original 80% reduction model. The Committee created a new range of scenarios, including a 'Balanced Net Zero' pathway reflecting aspects of all the modelled scenarios and showing a feasible but cautious way to achieve the target by 2050. The report was published in the same month that prime minister Johnson proposed a 68% cut in emissions by 2030, itself a highly ambitious target laid out a year before the UK's planned hosting of the CoP 26 climate change conference.

The sixth carbon budget had big news for aviation. For the first time, the CCC recommended that there should be no net capacity expansion at UK airports, 'unless the sector is on track to sufficiently outperform its net emissions trajectory and can accommodate the additional demand'.[53] In other words, significant progress must be made towards reducing emissions from the flights already in the skies above the UK before any new capacity with an inevitable increase in emissions is added. The CCC stated that expansion may be possible across the UK's national network of airports, but in line with the 'no net increase' line, any increase at one airport would necessarily mean a reduction in capacity for other UK airports. This seemed to directly challenge the claims that an expanded Heathrow would not affect passenger numbers at the network of regional airports, an important part of the government's regional 'levelling-up' agenda.

The biggest news of all was that for the first time the CCC finally recommended that IAS emissions be formally included in carbon budgets, the step which had evaded campaigners since the CCA 08 had been passed thirteen years previously. Including IAS should replace the 'headroom' policy. Aviation industry insiders had long argued that the old policy was as good as formally including IAS emissions, but the CCC described this as 'unsustainable'. The Committee urged the government to act and increase pressure on the industry to improve its decarbonisation performance.[54] If evidence was required of the problems caused by not including IAS emissions, the CCC pointed out that emissions from the aviation and shipping sectors would likely be a significant factor in the UK missing its targets for the fourth and fifth carbon budgets.

The message could not have been clearer. According to the government's independent climate advisors, aviation must now begin to contribute its fair share to reducing GHG emissions. The CCC also recommended a change in the planning assumption target for aviation. In order to meet the Balanced Net Zero pathway by 2050, UK aviation as a whole should reduce its emissions to 23MtCO2e by 2050, a significant reduction from the 37.5MtCO2e under the 80% target. The CCC still acknowledged that it was impossible for the sector to achieve zero emissions by 2050 owing to the technical issues involved in developing fully electrified planes and scaling up the production of sustainable fuels in time, so the remaining positive emissions in 2050 would need to be balanced out using engineered GHG removals. The CCC estimated that, without significant progress on decarbonisation, aviation would use up to a full 40% of the capacity available for offsetting across the whole economy.

Interestingly, the report also included modelling based on feedback from the UK's first Climate Assemblies, which had tested public opinion on the acceptability of various options for reducing carbon emissions. Climate Assemblies had been a key demand of Extinction Rebellion. In the inaugural sessions, participants were asked about a range of options for dealing with aviation emissions. The assemblies found that, when presented with impartial evidence, the participants had broadly supported the CCC's recommended constraining of demand increase to 25% above 2018 levels. This suggested that a cross-section of public opinion still felt that there was room for growth in the aviation market, but that unconstrained growth in demand while other sectors have to work harder was not acceptable. Based on feedback from the assemblies, the sixth carbon budget report concluded that a range of demand management policies might be acceptable to the public. These included carbon pricing, fuel duty, VAT on fares or reforms to Air Passenger Duty, and/or restricting the availability of flights through managing airport capacity. The assemblies also came out broadly in favour of the idea of some kind of frequent flyer levy, where those who travel more frequently should be expected to pay more towards the cost of emissions mitigation.

The government received the CCC's report. In April 2021 came the enormous news that the government had committed to formally including emissions from IAS in the UK's over-all carbon reduction targets. Along with an acceptance of the target of a 78% reduction in CO2 emissions by 2035, this was a major development. In July 2021 the government passed its Carbon Budget Order which effectively seals the commit-ments into law. It seemed as if aviation's free pass might be about to come to an end. If Heathrow was thinking it could argue in submitting a DCO for the third runway that it was not responsible for emissions from departing and arriving aircraft because aviation emissions were not included in the carbon budget, that would now have to change.

A week later, the Supreme Court judgment came in. The news was not good.

As we have seen, the previous stages had been solely con-cerned with the legality of the process behind the decisions made in drafting the ANPS. The judges at the Supreme Court stuck exactly to this question, in a move which some observers have suggested shows a willingness to demonstrate the institu-tion's independence from activist pressure for climate change action. The judgment was the climate lawyers' worst fear. The Supreme Court threw out all the judgments made at the Court of Appeal, and fully accepted Heathrow's grounds of appeal. In a unanimous decision, all five judges on the Supreme Court bench concluded that it had not been necessary to consider the Paris Agreement in drawing up the ANPS. Plan B's assertion that the 1.5°C limit had been government policy was rejected, along with FoE's case that a broader definition of sustainability needed to be adopted, and responsibilities for climate change after 2050 and non-CO2 warming ought to have been considered, under section 10 of the Planning Act.

In summary the judgment again boiled down to the strength of the UK's existing climate change legislation under CCA 08 and the bench taking a different view of the facts to the Court of Appeal. The Supreme Court's view was that the ANPS had been correctly designated in line with the existing carbon reduction target at that time. It viewed the reliance on domestic law as correct. The Paris Agreement was an unincorporated treaty, which should not have been considered. The CCC view that the CCA 08 80% limit was 'potentially consistent' with a range of temperature outcomes was again cited. In addition, the court stated that at the time the ANPS was designated the UK was required to submit its NDC as part of the European Union; but at that point the EU's NDC ambition was actually lower than the targets set by the CCA 08. This was effectively another reason not to consider Paris; in other words, under the EU's NDC, there would in fact have been *more* carbon budget available than under CCA 08.

With regards to Plan B's section 5 grounds, the judgment stated that Paris remained an unincorporated treaty, and overturned the Court of Appeal's significant ruling that 'government policy' did not have a special meaning in English. The court found that Crosland's examples were not strong enough: 'the statements concerning the development of policy which the Government made in 2018 were statements concerning an inchoate and developing policy and not an established policy to which section 5(8) refers';[55] it added that the anticipated government aviation decarbonisation strategy should provide some clarity on what this policy would be. On the broader duty under section 10, the Supreme Court held that it was not irrational for the Secretary of State to fail to model the expanded airport's emissions beyond 2050 when the policy relating to these longer-term emissions had yet to be decided. It found that this would be agreed when the new aviation strategy was published. Heathrow had contended that the excess emissions would be dealt with by a range of measures including improved efficiency, sustainable fuel and carbon pricing; all of this was evolving and would be included in its DCO application, which had been confirmed to be assessable against the Net Zero commitment. The judgment disagreed with Katie de Kauwe's key ground which had been accepted by the Court of Appeal, that the precautionary principle should apply in the event that there was a degree of continuing uncertainty regarding the impact of non-CO_2 warming. The court found that the DCO process should be expected to address these uncertainties and suggested that hopefully government would elaborate on this in the upcoming aviation strategy.

In drawing all these conclusions together, the Supreme Court reiterated the point that the ANPS and DCO process was robust, and that any DCO application made under the ANPS would be assessed against the climate obligations *as they stand at the time the application is made*. This meant that Heathrow Airport would have to show that its project was Net Zero-compliant, a much stricter limit than the 80% reduction target which was the accepted policy at the time of the ANPS designation. The court judged that this system was sophisticated enough to ensure that the impacts of planes in flight would be accounted for, and that any decision to grant a DCO allowing Heathrow to build the third runway would not lead to the UK breaching its international commitments on emissions reduction.

The Supreme Court judgment overturned the Court of Appeal judgment in its entirety. It established that considering the Paris Agreement was not necessary because CCA 08 was sufficient. It reinstated the ANPS, opening the way for Heathrow to now move to the next stage and apply for a DCO. 'This is the right result for the country,' said a Heathrow spokesperson, adding that the airport has already committed to Net Zero.[56]

It was a serious blow to campaigners, who had celebrated what felt like a breakthrough just a few months earlier. Many felt that the Supreme Court judgment reflected conservatism on the court benches, particularly after the political outcry that had followed the two Brexit Supreme Court decisions which had severely rebuked the government. Critics suggested that the court was keen not to appear to overtly challenge the government again. 'They can't bring themselves to admit what real climate action means for everything, all future infrastructure. Everything has to change. They're climate criminals,' said Nic Ferriday. 'It's outrageous to think that meeting climate commitments can be dealt with at planning stage – what lowly planning inspector is going to overrule the Supreme Court?'[57]

Did it really matter whether the reinstated ANPS was still based on the old 80% reduction target if the whole JR had clearly established that the DCO would be judged on the climate targets as they exist at the time of the application – which now would be Net Zero? Many planning lawyers believe that this is the correct approach because the national policy statement set out clear rules and planning processes are set out in legislation; leaving the details to the DCO stage means that national policies (NPSs) do not have to be rewritten every time there is a new technological or policy development. Moreover, the case showed that it is clear that in the DCO application a convincing plan would also have to be demonstrated for mitigating the emissions from planes in flight. The judgment was in no way a 'green light' for the third runway, Friends of the Earth argued.[58]

However, Cait Hewitt from the Aviation Environment Federation believes that the judgment sent completely the wrong message: 'it is the ultimate government policy approval', she says. 'It directly contradicts the government's own advisory body, the CCC, which had clearly stated that there should be no net expansion of UK airport capacity.'[59] The ANPS is designed to guide and assist planning inspectors and decision makers in assessing a DCO application. If the original ANPS was reinstated, and so explicitly endorsed the concept of airport expansion in the south-east as a policy for the future of the UK and recommended the north-west runway as the preferred scheme, it seems hard to see how the outcome of a DCO process would be to reject the third runway altogether.

The furore did not stop there. The evening before the Supreme Court judgment was officially issued on 16 December, Tim Crosland took many by surprise. He leaked the judgment on his Twitter feed, breaking a strict court embargo. In what he described as an 'act of civil disobedience' intended to draw attention to the climate crisis, he tweeted his disgust at the court's finding in favour of Heathrow Airport. Crosland argued that rather than acting out of frustration he had done it deliberately to protest at what he called the court's 'immoral' ruling. In February 2021 proceedings were issued against him by the Solicitor General for contempt of court, which is punishable by up to two years in prison and/or a fine. In defending his decision to leak the judgment, Crosland argued that his justification was that he had a strong belief that the Supreme Court judgment involved covering up vital evidence. In his opening submissions, he claimed that the final Supreme Court judgment made 'no reference' to the expectation that UK aviation would continue to emit 40MtCO2e per year in the event of a third runway being built. Nor did it mention the crucial admission that the government had indeed used the 2°C limit when deciding on the climate impacts of the third runway.[60] He argued that the court had left out these two key pieces of information because the judges understood that there was no way the third runway could be compatible with the UK's emission reduction commitments and that no-one assessing those targets against these commitments could have come to the conclusion that it was.

In early May 2021, Tim Crosland was convicted of contempt of court and ordered to pay a £5,000 fine and £15,000 in costs. He was unrepentant and launched an appeal against the conviction. This appeal failed in late 2021, although Crosland said he would take the case to the European Court of Human Rights. Reaction in the legal community was divided; some supported his fight, while others questioned why he would risk prison in a 'silly' move when the Supreme Court judgment would have been announced the next day anyway. Some felt he had taken a step too far, which threatened to divide the strategic environmental litigation community.

Paris is not relevant?

It had been a rollercoaster of a ride for the legal campaigners. Over eighteen months, the JR climate claimants had gone from losing on all grounds at the High Court to winning on all grounds at the Court of Appeal, to losing again on all grounds at the Supreme Court. In that time, the UK had moved to commit to Net Zero GHG emissions by 2050, and the CCC had recommended no new airport expansion in the UK.

The twists and turns of the case are hard to follow. The Court of Appeal's judgment in 2020 concluded that the Secretary of State had *not* taken the Paris Agreement into account, but the Supreme Court concluded that he had in fact considered it and decided to give it 'no weight'. This is even more perplexing because Heathrow's lawyers stated in the Supreme Court that Grayling had considered Paris, when the DfT had accepted the Court of Appeal judgment and decided not to appeal against it. Without the government arguing its side in the Supreme Court, Will Rundle says it was clear that 'the [Heathrow] appeal was even more clearly about commercial interests versus climate justice'.[61]

The judgment reconfirmed the primacy of the domestic targets. It reflected CCC advice that the CCA 08 80% reduction target was 'potentially consistent' with a range of temperature outcomes, and the 2016 advice against tougher measures to aim for a 1.5°C limit at that time. As the Supreme Court noted, if the government's own independent advisors had suggested that the 80% target need not yet be adjusted in line with the Paris aspiration (at least in 2016), then there was no need to consider the Paris Agreement. Furthermore, given the primacy of UK domestic law, the fact that Paris had yet to be incorporated led to the Civil Service legal advice which in turn led Chris Grayling and James Maurici to argue that Paris was not relevant, i.e. it would have been unlawful to take it into account.

This point that the CCA 08 was the correct law has been described as a 'fudge' by some observers. In effect, the Supreme Court avoided having to disagree with the Court of Appeal over whether the Paris Agreement was 'obviously material', which in legal terms means it must be taken into account. Instead, its judgment focused on the status of the Paris Agreement as an unincorporated treaty and the advice that this made it 'not relevant'. Barrister Pete Lockley points out that in fact the Supreme Court judgment does not challenge the Court of Appeal's conclusion on what 'obviously material' means. He argues that by establishing what appears to be a rather small technical point, there is now the possibility of exploring in future litigation what 'obviously material' means in relation to the Paris Agreement. 'The smart thing for a lawyer is to show the minimum error, and not to get bogged down in complex wider points,' he told me over Zoom.[62]

At the same time, Craig Bennett believes that the real importance of the court case is not the final judgment, but winning in the court of public opinion: 'I really believe that you win even when you lose,' he told me.[63] There certainly seemed to be a symbolic victory in the Heathrow JR. As we shall see in Chapter 5, the Court of Appeal judgment and the strategy of testing whether NPSs for national infrastructure projects were still fit for purpose in a Net Zero world have influenced a number of other similar judicial review challenges which were launched around the same time. And perhaps most importantly for the climate campaigners, there has been another delay. The third runway is still not a reality and certainly looks a long way off (for now). 'We wanted to raise the investment and political risk of expanding Heathrow,' says Bennett. 'The longer this goes on, the climate arguments will only become more important, the numbers will make even less sense, and Heathrow Airport may lose the public licence to operate.'[64]

4

EMINENTLY FIXABLE

During the course of writing this book, I have tried to get a detailed interview with a representative of Heathrow Airport in order to understand their thinking on how to tackle the inevitable increased carbon emissions from airport expansion. This is key information which would form a part of the company's expected DCO application. Despite several approaches, I was unable to arrange an interview, either via the press office or via the director of sustainability, Matt Gorman, who received an MBE for his services to sustainability in 2021. This leaves me to rely on publicly available documents to understand what Heathrow Airport thinks it is responsible for, and the mitigation approaches it may propose.

Does the aviation industry think that carbon budgets don't *really* apply to flying? Was this behind Heathrow Airport Limited's breezy assertion when the Supreme Court judgment was announced, that the apparent contradictions in reconciling expansion plans with ever-tightening carbon budgets were 'eminently fixable'?

This chapter attempts to examine some of the approaches the developer may take in order to mitigate the impact of expansion on the UK's carbon budgets, and steps the aviation industry in general may take towards decarbonisation. As we have seen, the Heathrow JR conclusively established that any DCO applicant would be responsible for showing the carbon impacts of not just the airport infrastructure, but the actual planes in flight, and convincing plans for how those emissions should be mitigated. The second key gain from the legal action was that any DCO applicant would be working to Net Zero by 2050, with aviation allowed an exceptional 23MtCO2e residual emissions budget by that date.

Reading Heathrow's airport expansion consultation documents from 2018, there is a heavy reliance on technological and efficiency improvements, and carbon pricing approaches, to override the impact of the inevitable increased emissions caused by a quarter of a million extra planes landing at the airport every year. The document seems predicated on business as usual at the airport, just with a few more technical fixes.

International efforts

As we have seen, aviation has a peculiar position because of its international nature. Previous disagreements over where GHG emissions should be accounted for, plus fears that unilateral measures in one country would lead to 'carbon leakage', meant that when the CCA 08 was drawn up it was recommended that aviation should be subject to international processes to promote decarbonisation of the industry globally. Over the years, the CCC began to develop this message to include domestic measures a government could take, but before 2020 it stopped short of recommending the inclusion of aviation emissions in carbon budgets.

Heathrow Airport has long advertised its participation in and support of global schemes which aim to reduce aviation's impacts. These schemes broadly employ what are known as market-based measures: purchasing carbon offsets (discussed below) or trading permits to emit carbon on an open market. The main international scheme, CORSIA, runs through the ICAO and its main policy measure is the use of carbon offsets to achieve the relatively unambitious target of carbon-neutral growth in the industry from 2020 onwards. Note that CORSIA is not aiming to reduce actual emissions, just attempt to stop adding any more even as aviation hopes to expand globally. IATA recommends the CORSIA scheme to its members along with technical and efficiency improvements in its four pillars of mitigation for climate change impacts from aviation.[1]

The other scheme which affected UK aviation until the end of 2020 was the EU ETS, which is significantly more ambitious than CORSIA. The EU ETS is the world's first and biggest carbon market, covering about 40% of Europe's CO_2 emissions. The ETS creates a limited quantity of allowances, and over time these are reduced so that emissions will fall eventually to nothing. Emitters are allowed to buy or sell allowances depending on the extent to which they meet reductions targets; the limit on the number of the permits means that the market then decides their value, one aspect of the carbon price. The EU argues that 'trading brings flexibility that ensures that emissions are cut where it costs least to do so',[2] and believes that market signals should then drive investment in low-carbon technologies.

Since 2012, the EU ETS has included all international aviation operating within the European Economic Area, but does not include flights from outside Europe. The ETS

Directive was amended in 2021 and the bloc committed to supporting CORSIA, to try to improve the UN scheme in line with the EU's objective of a 55% cut in emissions by 2030. At the time of writing the EU ETS continues to apply only to flights operating within Europe. The bloc-wide carbon price was around €90 a tonne in early 2022. For context, some of the modelling in the Airports Commission documents assumed a carbon price of £330 a tonne would be needed to dampen demand on aviation sufficiently to stay within the CCC's planning assumption for aviation.

Things were complicated further by Brexit, and as of the end of 2020 the UK formally left the EU ETS. In January 2021 the UK replaced the scheme with its own UK ETS which essentially retained a number of key features of the EU system.[3] Aviation continues to be subject to cap and trade policies. Early indications suggest that the scheme may in fact go further than the EU option, because the UK's current climate ambition is higher than the EU's. The cap on the allowances will be set at 5% below the UK's share under the EU rules and, overall, the UK is aiming to reduce emissions by 68% by 2030 while the EU is only aiming for 55%. At the time of writing, no analysis of the effectiveness of this scheme is available.

A word on offsetting

In October 1517, Martin Luther, professor of moral philosophy at Wittenberg University, posted his ninety-five theses or *Disputation on the Power and Efficacy of Indulgences* on a church door in Wittenberg. The document outlined what Luther saw as abuse by the clergy of the practice of selling indulgences on behalf of the papacy, certificates believed to reduce the time a soul needed to spend in purgatory atoning for temporal sins. These indulgences were known as part of the 'economy of salvation'. Penitents confessed their sin and then performed good works to atone. But Luther became enraged that, in the exchange of money for effectively being let off the sin, the true message of Christ was being obfuscated. When Luther's theses were reprinted this set off a pamphlet war with the man seen as a chief promoter of indulgences, Johann Tetzel. Luther was excommunicated for his criticism, sparking the seismic changes in Christianity that led to the establishment of the Protestant faith.

It goes without saying that taking a flight is not as morally bad as murder, theft or adultery. But many have argued that carbon offsets, if done badly, represent a version of a modern-day papal indulgence – paying money to make a problem go away. Most airlines now offer passengers the option at the point of ticket sale to purchase an offset to mitigate the carbon impact of the flight they are planning to take, sometimes referred to as 'guilt-free flying'. Some of these offsets cost just a couple of pounds, and promise nothing more than to plant a tree, which may or may not happen and may or may not offset any carbon (see below). Even the CEO of European carrier Wizz Air said offsetting was 'a bit of a joke'.[4]

What exactly is an offset? There are broadly two types – nature-based approaches and encouraging and paying someone else not to emit CO_2. Trees and, increasingly, restored peatlands and improved soil can absorb significant amounts of carbon dioxide. There are also geological techniques that have yet to be tested on a mass scale, such as advanced weathering of rock – limestone can react with sea water to convert CO_2 to alkaline bicarbonate; in the oceans this safely sinks to the seabed. Large amounts of CO2 are also absorbed by healthy oceans around the world, through photosynthesis and other processes. Tree planting, and its sister approaches rewilding, regenerative agriculture and afforestation, are valuable tools and have historically been used as a form of offset. The CCC acknowledges that we will not be able to achieve our 2050 targets without creating significant new areas of forest, and indeed ceasing to cut down the trees that we already have. The second type of offsets are a kind of official credit which can be bought or sold between polluters such as airlines. This effectively rewards third parties for reducing their emissions or for carrying out projects which will reduce or remove emissions. For example, airlines can gain emissions credits by financially contributing to the establishment of a wind farm in another country, or supporting a factory to reduce its energy intensity.

However, offsetting has become increasingly discredited. A study for the European Commission found that 87% of over 5,000 carbon offset projects were 'not delivering the CO2 reductions they were certified for'.[5] Planting a tree today and claiming that the tree should be able to remove a set amount of CO2 over its lifetime is one thing, but there is no guarantee that the tree will still be alive in 100 years' time. Tree planting does not immediately mean carbon-neutrality; in the early years tree survival rates depend heavily on where and how they are planted and trees perform relatively little photosynthesis until they mature, which takes time. A tree may be cut down, die in a wildfire or lose its ability to absorb carbon because the climate is now too hot, cold or wet to support it. The European Commission report was particularly critical of projects which are not 'additional'; which would have happened anyway. For an offset to add to the net mitigation of emissions, it must be clear that the project would *not* have happened in the absence of a market for offset credits.

It is also incorrect to think of offsets as neutralising new emissions from a new activity. To make this simple, if a passenger's share of a flight's emissions equals one tonne of CO2, and the passenger pays someone else not to emit a tonne of CO2 by purchasing a credit offset, the net result is still one tonne of CO2 being emitted, not zero tonnes. 'The idea that offsetting makes a tonne of CO2 from aviation "neutral" is misleading; if an offset pays for an emissions reduction that needs to happen anyway then that tonne of CO2 emitted from the aircraft will still cause warming and be inconsistent with a "net zero" climate goal', argues the Aviation Environment Federation.[6] Again, if the offset (or tree planting) simply matches the emission, it will do nothing to draw down the excess carbon already in the atmosphere.

The CCC Net Zero report in 2019 quite clearly recommended that the use of offsets should be minimised. 'Most sectors will need to reduce emissions close to zero without offsetting; the target cannot be met by simply adding mass removal of CO2 onto existing plans for the 80% target,' it states. However, the report recommends that offsets may be used as an interim measure to help decarbonise sectors such as aviation, but that they must not be relied on over and above actions that actually reduce emissions. In short, aviation needs to offset *and* reduce its emissions.

SAF, electric aircraft and efficiency gains

Much has been written about the potential for 'sustainable aviation fuels' to reduce emissions from flying. SAF is a catch-all term that covers everything from conventional biofuels, to fuels made from waste, to synthetic fuels or electrofuels. There has been much research and development in the area in recent years with the growing realisation that fully electrifying aviation remains a distant dream, especially for long-haul flights. Hybrid aircraft may become feasible before 2050, but fully electric planes will take large amounts of development money to get off the ground, going through multiple rounds of safety testing and being affected by the slow turnover of the world aviation fleet by airlines.

Biofuels are at the most advanced stage of development. They are derived from alternative sources to petroleum, for example plants, woody biomass or waste vegetable oils. They are considered to be sustainable because, although they emit around the same quantity of CO_2 as conventional fuels as they combust during flight, those emissions are considered to be offset by the CO_2 the plant absorbed while it was alive. This is considered to form a closed loop (in emissions terms), but as we have seen with the arguments against offsetting, a fuel can only claim to be sustainable if the amount the plant absorbs perfectly matches the quantity of CO_2 emitted when the fuel is burned. How can we be sure that this will occur at all, and if it does, continue indefinitely into the future?

Biofuels got off to a good start as a renewable approach for all forms of transport fuel, with the EU and others giving subsidies towards production. They were particularly popular as they could be used as 'drop-in' fuels, meaning they could be blended with kerosene without aircraft engines needing to be adjusted for their use. However, research soon showed that dedicating huge areas of land to the production of palm oil, and latterly soy, was driving deforestation (in itself releasing huge amounts of CO2), and threatened to take agricultural land out of production which would drive up food prices. One estimate put the land required to produce enough biofuels to meet 50% of the EU's aviation needs by 2050 at 33m hectares, or roughly the size of Finland.[7] Burning crops such as rape seed and corn starch for fuel instead of producing food for people was widely criticised, and the production of the fuels also used large amounts of water. In 2019 the EU ruled that biofuels derived from palm oil could no longer be labelled sustainable.

Research then moved on to look at 'second generation' biofuels which were made from materials not usually regarded as food, such as algae or food waste. Some of these fuels are now at an advanced stage of development, but quick roll-out continues to be restricted by the small scale of commercial production and competition for the raw material from other industries. These advanced biofuels are therefore more expensive than conventional fuels, around twice as expensive according to one estimate.[8]

Electrofuels, or 'power-to-liquid' fuels, are created when electricity is used to produce a liquid hydrocarbon that can be burned in an internal combustion engine. A subset of these fuels is known as E-kerosene which combines hydrogen and CO_2. For these fuels to be considered carbon-neutral, the electricity applied needs to be produced from sources that are 100% renewable and 'additional' – i.e. producers should not use electricity which would otherwise be used to decarbonise other sectors of the economy. The CO_2 inputs need to be captured from the air, which can be considered as carbon removal, but this is also an energy-intensive process. There has been some excitement over the development of these fuels, and research describes the concept as promising, particularly for industries such as aviation which are hard to decarbonise. However, *Transport and Environment* research shows that on current projections, delivering 50% of the EU energy demands for aviation by 2050 would require 24% of the currently available renewable energy production and 8m hectares of land.[9]

SAF will have an important role to play in decarbonising aviation, but there continues to be disagreement about just how significant this will be. The renewable energy and land requirements are significant hurdles that need to be overcome before these fuels can be produced on a mass scale at a competitive price. At the same time, due to the slow production of aircraft and low rates of replacement, it will take time for planes which operate most efficiently on these fuels to make a significant contribution to reducing emissions. Key steps also need to be taken to ensure that the fuels can convincingly be described as carbon-neutral. To meet the energy needs of an *expanded* aviation sector by 2050, enormous amounts of money and production capacity needs to be brought online very quickly and at low cost, and the scaling up of renewable electricity production sites needs to not be at the expense of farmland or habitats or forests. For these reasons, the CCC's analysis of the role that SAF will play in decarbonising aviation by 2050 is circumspect, contributing to '25% of liquid fuel consumed in 2050, with just over two-thirds of this coming from biofuels and the remainder from carbon-neutral synthetic jet fuel (produced via direct air capture of CO_2 combined with low-carbon hydrogen)'.[10] Nevertheless, there is still much interest in the role SAF can play and a hope that the government will subsidise production and provide a mandate for a significant quantity of SAF to be included in the aviation energy mix in the future.

There has been similar excitement about the development of fully electric and hybrid electric planes. A 2019 report by Citigroup said that the development of small electric planes and 'electric air taxis' was moving fast and predicted that electric jets would begin disrupting the regional air market (flights up to 1,000 miles) by 2030.[11] A number of successful test flights have taken place, some using planes powered entirely by solar cells. However, other commentators are more circumspect. At issue is the enormous quantity and density of energy required to get a fully laden plane into the sky – it is not as simple as electrifying a relatively light urban vehicle. This is compounded by the extra weight of the large electric batteries which the planes would require. Electric planes have typically flown at slower speeds than jet planes, meaning that passengers may need to accept longer journey times and probably increased ticket prices to cover the cost of technical development. For these reasons, British Airways' chief executive predicted that it was unlikely that electrified planes would make a significant entry into the market before 2050, and instead backed the development of SAF, which might make up 'a third' of jet fuel by 2050.[12]

The final measure to be considered is efficiency gains, in particular those stemming from airspace modernisation improvements. The government's Jet Zero strategy of July 2021 (see below) estimates that historical efficiency gains through improved use of fuel savings techniques and newer aircraft can increase from 1.5% per annum to 2%. Airspace modernisation involves changing some of the routes that aircraft use in the sky and measures such as real-time information to pilots which would allow them to speed up or slow down as they approach an airport, removing the need to enter holding patterns as they wait for a landing slot to become available. Overall, the strategy expects that, by 2050, at least 25% of the CO_2 savings that it predicts for the aviation sector could come from these improvements. And yet like all the technological approaches I have analysed so far (wait for it), there is of course a 'but': creating more available air space theoretically frees up capacity which could be taken up by more planes emitting more CO_2.

So how can a basket of the measures outlined above help to mitigate the impact of emissions from UK aviation to 2050? In particular how effective would those measures be in limiting the impact of the increased emissions from a third runway at Heathrow Airport, and ensuring that adding 240,000 flights a year to the schedule does not put the UK's climate targets in jeopardy? Not surprisingly, there is some divergence between the recommendations of the CCC and the plans of the aviation industry.

Balanced Net Zero pathway

In its sixth carbon budget the CCC's recommended pathway for reducing emissions from aviation puts demand management front and centre. It is the first suggestion discussed in detail in the report, which outlines a mix of a robust carbon price and taxation measures feeding through to higher ticket prices which will eventually discourage flying. The second and third recommendations in the report are improvements in efficiency – including the use of hybrid electric aeroplanes – and uptake in the use of SAF. The report models a number of scenarios, testing different levels of adoption of each of the measures – for example, looking at how a faster roll-out of SAF might affect the need to reduce passenger numbers.

In the Balanced Net Zero pathway, what the CCC considers to be the most achievable scenario, demand prior to 2050 is restricted to a 25% increase on 2018 levels. Crucially, this involves no additional airport capacity: 'there should be no net expansion of UK airport capacity unless the sector is on track to sufficiently outperform its net emissions trajectory and can accommodate the additional demand'. The report notes that the current capacity of all the UK's airports together is 370m passengers per year, and a 25% increase in passenger numbers through Heathrow would amount to 365m passengers per year. The committee notes that expansion could be allowed at other airports, but only if capacity is reduced somewhere in the national network of airports. The scenarios modelled to manage that demand involve either putting up taxes on aviation, or restrictions on capacity. The taxation options include a frequent flyer levy, introducing fuel duty or VAT, or reforms to Air Passenger Duty. The availability of flights could be restricted by managing airport capacity, essentially through the use of air traffic control.

In this Balanced pathway, the CCC recommends that there should be increased support for SAF, including funding towards development costs and the construction of commercial production facilities. The scenario calls for 25% of fuel use to come from SAF by 2050 – two-thirds of this from sustainable biofuels and the remainder from carbon-neutral synthetic jet fuel. Efficiency gains should increase to 1.4% per year (compared to 0.7% in the baseline model), with 9% of total aircraft distance being flown by hybrid electric planes by 2050. On this pathway, emissions from aviation decline slowly from 37.5 $MtCO2e$ in 2018 to $23MtCO2e$ in 2050, which would still take up a considerable amount of the UK's carbon budget in the latter year. The CCC states that these residual emissions would need to be balanced out by GHG removals technologies.

How the industry plans to square the circle on emissions

Sustainable Aviation UK (SA UK) is a coalition of airlines, airports, manufacturers, air navigation services and business partners established in 2005 to tackle 'the challenge of ensuring a cleaner, quieter, smarter future for our industry'. It claims to represent 90% of the aviation industry, including all the UK's main airports and carriers such as BA and Virgin. In February 2020, just before the verdict in the Appeals Court stage of the Heathrow JR, the alliance pledged to make flying 'Net-Zero by 2050'. Significantly, SA UK claimed this would still be possible without any real constraints on growth in the number of flights or passenger numbers – in fact the alliance simultaneously announced it was still planning for a 70% increase in flights (or an extra 100m passengers a year) over the same time scale.[13]

The Net Zero commitment was an important step, as previously the industry had only been committed to a 50% reduction. Some of the measures proposed by SA UK mirrored recommendations from the CCC, including increasing uptake of SAF (although the plan had this making up a larger share of reductions – up to a third of fuel use by 2050), fuel efficiency measures, technological advances in engine design and airspace modification. But as the ambition to increase passenger numbers shows, the industry body does not agree with the key recommendation of the CCC to use carbon pricing and taxation measures to substantially dampen demand growth.

Recall that the DfT projected UK aviation would generate 40MtCO2e in 2050 with an expanded Heathrow. In its
calculations, the SA UK 'roadmap' assumes a baseline of
71MtCO2e will be emitted by the UK aviation sector in 2050
if nothing is done to mitigate emissions; obviously well above
the CCC's original 37.5MtCO2e and even further beyond the
residual 23MtCO2e under Net Zero. The report then goes on
to outline how the industry plans to mitigate this. Importantly,
SA UK sees only a small role for demand-side measures which
would only account for reducing 4Mt of CO2 by 2050, or
roughly 5.6% of the total they predict. Efficiency gains, such as
flying more direct routes and avoiding 'stacking', and developing the roll-out of SAF would provide 57% of the reductions.[14]
Crucially, despite the bad press and all the limitations laid out
above, offsetting of the industry's emissions was to play a significant role in the calculations. SA UK envisages about 25Mt
(35% of the savings) generated annually to be 'balanced out'
through nature-based approaches and paying others not to pollute in other sectors of the economy.

Many commentators praised the SA UK plan, but it was
dismissed as greenwashing by campaign groups such as
Greenpeace. Some of the accounting measures, such as the
heavy reliance on offsets, were criticised by analysts. Gwyn
Topham writing in *The Guardian* described the plan to constrain
demand to an increase of 70% as 'jiggery-pokery'.[15] SA UK's
own literature, perhaps inadvertently, indicates the scale of
the challenge. 'Between 2005 and 2016 Sustainable Aviation's
member airlines carried 26% more passengers and freight
but only grew absolute CO2 emissions by 9%,' showing that
although there had been some decoupling of emissions growth
from economic growth in the sector, there was certainly nothing

indicating that emissions from the sector had even begun to fall, as required by the recommendations of the CCC.

What of Heathrow's plans? The Supreme Court judgment in late 2020 effectively cleared the way for the airport to begin drawing up its application for a DCO under the terms of the original ANPS. Recall, however, that this judgment also established that the DCO would be assessed on climate laws as they are at the time of the application – carbon targets are not 'frozen'. It also established that carbon emissions from planes using the airport must be included in any analysis of the effects on the carbon budget, and that the developer would need to make a convincing argument that this was feasible. This seemed like a solid conclusion that would significantly raise the bar for a developer. How could it be argued that an extra 700 flights a day, and DfT estimates that UK aviation would still be generating 40MtCO2e per year in 2050 with a third runway, be squared with the need to meet Net Zero by 2050?

Much of what Heathrow might be thinking is outlined in key documents such as the 'Heathrow 2.0: Carbon neutral growth roadmap' and the company's expansion consultation document of 2018. Heathrow 2.0 outlines four steps – accelerating the roll-out of new aircraft, modernising airspace, encouraging the uptake of SAF and promoting carbon pricing and 'best practice' offsetting.[16] The document is clear that the main focus – like that of CORSIA – should be on ensuring that *growth* of the airport is carbon-neutral: 'growth in emissions from additional flights after expansion would be offset through carbon credits – resulting in no net growth in emissions'. There is no mention of reducing the baseline of emissions, or responsibility for emissions already emitted. The strategy outlines a number of incentives the airport could offer to encourage the development of electric aircraft, such as offering lower landing charges for airlines which use lower-carbon planes. Importantly, the document makes no secret that a significant part of its objective would be achieved through the 'purchase [of] carbon credits' from other sectors. This may lead to higher prices as the cost of the credits would be passed on to passengers. It emphasises that the company supported the inclusion of emissions from flights in the EU ETS from 2012.

In addition, Heathrow Airport has been widely praised for its commitment to investing in 'nature-based solutions' for carbon removal. The airport has invested £94,000 in a project in Lancashire to restore 70 hectares of peatland. Of the UK's peatland, 80% is degraded after years of cutting and draining, and this can cause it to emit carbon. Blocking drainage ditches and replanting sphagnum mosses can help stop this carbon leakage. However, it is important to understand that this does not mean the same thing as soaking up the carbon which is being emitted right now from planes arriving every couple of minutes at Heathrow. Some areas of UK peatland are so degraded it may take many years for them to begin to absorb carbon again, and many more than that before they start to be able to sequester large amounts. In fact, one of the aims of peatland restoration is simply to stop the most degraded areas from just *emitting* carbon in the first place. There are legitimate concerns that in fifty years' time climate change itself may disrupt weather patterns so severely that the peat may never be able to sequester carbon again in significant amounts. Some environmental analysts, including the consultancy Futerra, have praised Heathrow's carbon-neutral plan for bringing to the fore some of the more innovative solutions to climate change, but the Aviation Environment Federation claimed that it offered few new ideas and was particularly critical about the heavy reliance on offsets.[17]

Importantly, Heathrow 2.0 suggests that, at least in 2018, the airport did not consider itself to be responsible for the emissions of aircraft in flight, which make up 95% of the emissions associated with the airport:[18] 'Heathrow does not design aircraft, fly planes or make aviation fuel – and does not control the businesses that do'. The document lays out some measures which may make up parts of the DCO application, and these are clearly restricted to measures affecting only the operation of the new terminal – for example, changing to low-energy lightbulbs and switching to electric service vehicles on the tarmac. Further measures are proposed to modernise air space management, avoiding stacking and holding patterns which waste fuel, as well as to encourage passengers to travel to the terminal buildings via public transport. The carbon-neutral growth roadmap established that the airport will support international measures such as CORSIA and the EU ETS, and 'show leadership' through joining bodies such as SA UK to look for ways to design a sustainable aviation roadmap.

An AEF analysis of the plan was scathing:

> Delivery of the carbon neutral pledge will in fact require almost no action from Heathrow. While many of the initiatives described are worthwhile, there is hardly anything in the plan that is additional to what's happening anyway: almost all the proposed actions involve Heathrow riding on the coattails of other Government or industry initiatives.[19]

Heathrow's third runway consultation documents give a further clear indication of where the DCO application may focus. This document was last updated in 2019 and outlines four broad areas: mitigation measures in construction design, air transport (offsetting, efficiency, avoiding stacking), surface access and airport buildings. As we have seen it makes it as clear as it can be that the airport did not at this point believe itself responsible for mitigating emission from planes taking off and landing. This was because the UK carbon budgets at that time did not include emissions from IAS.

> Our assessment ... excludes Greenhouse Gas emissions from international aviation, which are not included in current UK carbon budgets or explicitly in the UK's 2050 target. ... Expansion at Heathrow is not considered to materially affect the ability of the Government to meet UK carbon reduction targets.[20]

There is a deeper point to consider. While Heathrow will no doubt hire the brightest and the best to quantify the precise impacts of its mitigation efforts on the increased carbon emissions from the third runway, is it right that a private company operated in the interests of foreign shareholders should be making arguments about the overall balance of the UK's CO2 emissions? If the job of the DCO application is to show that 240,000 extra planes a year will not add to the total amount of carbon emitted, should we be allowing Heathrow Airport to assess how effective emissions reductions strategies in other sectors of the economy are? Will the company have the correct information about how road transport will have decarbonised by 2050, or agriculture? Would it even have reliable information about what its competitor airports – Gatwick, Bristol, Southampton, etc. – are planning? If the expansion plans do ever progress to consideration of the DCO, it is vital that the officials charged with analysing the proposals have clear and unbiased access to this information. And the NGOs who will no doubt challenge the process and how these calculations are made will need deep pockets and plenty of time.

Jet Zero

In July 2021 the Johnson government finally published its long-awaited draft aviation decarbonisation strategy, which has become known as Jet Zero. The document's publication had been repeatedly delayed over two years due to the coronavirus pandemic. Jet Zero has been drawn up through consultation with the 'Jet Zero council', a joint government/industry body charged with delivering a plan for net zero CO_2 aviation by 2050. There had been much speculation in the aviation community about what the document might say about expanding Heathrow Airport, and whether the strategy would reflect the CCC recommendations that demand management be the number one policy option for the government, followed by developing SAF and efficiency improvements. The CCC had also recommended against any increase in net airport capacity until there had been significant progress in decarbonising aviation.

In a move which failed to surprise campaigners, the Jet Zero consultation document was remarkably light on policies to constrain even *growth* in demand, directly contradicting the CCC recommendations. The document has five recommendations – strategies for developing hybrid and electric aircraft; airspace modernisation; increasing the amount of SAF used by the aviation industry to 30% of fuel in 2050, from the current projected usage of 5%; using emissions-capping market mechanisms, offsets and removals such as DACCS; and last but (presumably) by no means least, 'influencing consumers' to make sustainable travel choices. The last recommendation includes a proposal to publish carbon emissions information at the point of purchasing a flight ticket. The CCC's recommendation (no net expansion) was largely airbrushed out: 'the industry's need to rebuild from a lower base [after the pandemic] is likely to mean that plans for airport expansion will be slower to come forward' was the only reference. There is no explicit indication that the government plans to follow the CCC's recommendation to restrict demand.

There were some moves in the Jet Zero document which campaigners welcomed. The document proposes to decarbonise domestic flights in the UK by 2040, and there is also a plan to set five-yearly targets for emissions reduction from the sector to 2050. Interestingly, additional non-CO2 warming impacts of aviation are mentioned in Jet Zero, but the proposals on actions are vague, and the strategy continues to refer to 'a large degree of uncertainty' over the exact scale of the effect. In its 'high ambition' scenario, the document models GHG emissions being reduced to a residual 23MtCO2e by 2050 with the most significant reductions coming through fuel efficiency improvements and the increased use of SAF.

At heart the Jet Zero strategy appears to be an exposition of a techno-optimistic view of how to mitigate emissions to avoid the worst impacts of climate change. The text is at pains to avoid recommending that there should be any constraints to demand growth at all. Jet Zero is keen to promote the benefits of flying and is careful to not undermine the obvious confidence that the aviation industry has in the technological fixes. In fact, aviation minister Rachel McClean was quoted as saying that people had to 'keep flying' in order to save the planet, to encourage the industry to have the confidence to invest in the new technologies[21] (although she was moved to the Home Office two days later following a Cabinet reshuffle).

The Jet Zero strategy does acknowledge that many of these proposed new technologies – electric planes and industry-scale

GHG removals such as DACCS and BECCS – are still in their 'infancy'. For example, to date only one DACCS plant has come into operation, in Iceland, with a capacity to remove a mere 4,000 tonnes of CO2 per year. This is equivalent to just half of some estimates of what one individual using a private jet can contribute each year.[22] We have seen in earlier sections the difficulties involved in relying on these technologies being deployed at scale in the future, perhaps as soon as fifteen or twenty years from now, and there may be significant costs involved. We have seen that even the aviation industry does not believe that a zero-emission aircraft that does not rely on offsets or SAF will be in operation before 2050, except on some short-haul routes. Faith in these technologies cannot replace the need to reduce actual emissions from all sectors today.

It seems that without naming Heathrow Airport explicitly, the current government is not yet willing to publicly ask the aviation industry to do anything significant to constrain demand for flying. However, in October 2021, when the government published its plan to get the whole economy on track for Net Zero, a document from the 'Nudge unit' at BEIS was also published. This recommended the use of social influences to help reduce demand for flying, but the document was hastily deleted.[23] If further confirmation of the government's view on aviation growth was needed, look no further than the introduction to the Net Zero strategy: 'in 2050, we will still be … flying planes,' writes Boris Johnson, who had once threatened to lie down in front of the bulldozers if Heathrow expansion was given the green light, 'but our planes will be zero emission allowing us to fly guilt-free'.[24]

LOSE THE BATTLE, WIN THE WAR

There is no doubt that the Supreme Court ruling overturning the Court of Appeal's decision in December 2020 was a severe blow to campaigners. Having been tantalisingly close to a precedent on the importance of the Paris Agreement, the Supreme Court judgment snatched defeat from the jaws of victory. It set a cautious tone for the evolution of strategic climate litigation. 'The Supreme Court did what a conservative court would do,' says Joana Setzer from LSE. 'But the case still showed how concerned people are. They nearly won, and that was scary for the government.'[1]

Despite this final ruling reinstating the ANPS, the Heathrow JR has still had a significant impact in the UK and came at a time when strategic climate litigation is growing in importance. The arguments explored in the Heathrow JR informed, influenced and resonated with arguments used in a number of similar cases which were filed and were being heard around the same time. These cases all argued in slightly different ways that decisions on national infrastructure projects are legally required to consider the effects of the projects' GHG emissions on the UK's climate change commitments. As we have seen, since the 2019 Net Zero decision, these commitments reflect the Paris Agreement 1.5°C temperature limit. Some of the cases involved exploring the 2008 Planning Act and its provisions on climate change, some looked more specifically at the Paris Agreement and others explored the impacts of carbon reduction targets if aviation expansion under the reinstated ANPS was allowed to go ahead.

'What are your influences, man?'

The first of these cases was filed in January 2020, three weeks before the appeals court judgment in the Heathrow JR. This case involved the Energy National Policy Statement (ENPS), another foundational planning document like the ANPS, and was filed by Client Earth. The case requested a JR into the 2019 decision to grant a DCO under the ENPS for two new gas-fired power generation units at the giant Drax power station near Selby in East Yorkshire, which had previously burned coal to produce electricity. The Planning Inspectorate had recommended that the DCO should not be granted because it would jeopardise the UK's commitments under the CCA 08; Client Earth argued in court that when fully operational the 3.6GW plant would be responsible for 75% of the UK's total carbon emissions. However, Andrea Leadsom, then Secretary of State at BEIS, had overruled the planning inspector and approved the project. She had argued that Drax would represent a transitional solution, balancing out gaps in an unreliable supply of renewable energy. She argued that the needs of consumers must be balanced against carbon reduction requirements. The first attempt by Client Earth failed. In rejecting Client Earth's case, Mr Justice Holgate at the Divisional Court said that the Energy

NPS, designated in 2011, clearly established the need for continuing reliance on fossil fuels, even if they have significant impacts on carbon emissions. The judge recommended that the appropriate procedure to challenge whether the Energy NPS is still correct in light of the UK's new Net Zero commitments (in response to the Paris Agreement) would be through requesting a statutory review under the 2008 Planning Act.

This decision led to another case. Campaigners George Monbiot and the Ecotricity founder Dale Vince took Mr Justice Holgate's advice. They were represented by the Good Law Project (which had a headline success in February 2021 with its JR into the awarding of contracts for personal protective equipment in the early days of the COVID-19 pandemic). This application for a JR, launched in May 2020, focused on the ENPS. As Mr Justice Holgate had noted, this document envisaged that fossil fuels would play 'a significant role in years to come …', clearing the way for planning applications based on fracking shale gas, gas-fired power plants or new open-cast coal mines. The ENPS, which included a sub-NPS specifically on fossil fuels (EN2), was designated in 2011. The GLP case rested on section 6 3(a) of the Planning Act which stipulates that the minister for BEIS has a duty to consider reviewing the NPS if the circumstances surrounding the designation of the NPS have changed:

> Since the time when the statement was first published or (if later) last reviewed, there has been a significant change in any circumstances on the basis of which any of the policy set out in the statement was decided.[2]

Now that the Paris Agreement 1.5°C temperature limit had been reflected in the new Net Zero target, it was hard to argue that there had not been a significant change in the climate emissions reduction landscape. However, pre-trial correspondence disclosed to the court from civil servants revealed that 'the Secretary of State had never personally thought about whether to review the policy'.[3] At the same time there was evidence that civil servants had failed to refer the question whether to review the ENPS to the Secretary of State after 2018, despite the sea change in the UK's legal requirements. This formed an important element of the GLP case.

The court documents reveal how the case drew on the outcome of the Airports ANPS victory at the Appeals Court, just a few months previously. The background court documents also reference section 5 of the Planning Act 2008, which had formed the backbone of Plan B's successful appeal. There was also reference to the minister's duties under section 10 of the Planning Act and the need to ensure that planning policy promotes sustainable development. The claimants also argued that the ENPS should be declared to have no legal effect until a review was carried out, asking for a remedy that would be similar to what had occurred to the ANPS just a few months earlier.[4]

This time the strategy worked. Just a few days before the results of the GLP JR claim were announced in October 2020, the lawyers received a letter that confirmed that the minister at BEIS, then Alok Sharma, had verbally committed to a provisional decision to review the ENPS. Sharma would go on to preside over the UK's hosting of CoP26 in Glasgow. His decision to review the ENPS was confirmed in a much-anticipated Energy White Paper which was published in December 2020.

The key foundational document for all future energy infrastructure projects in the UK would now be reviewed in the light of the Net Zero commitments, a clear win for campaigners. The victory was tempered by the fact that in May 2020 the Court of Appeal again rejected Client Earth's earlier case challenging the granting of the DCO to Drax under the original ENPS, but this was not the end of the story. In a further significant development, in February 2021, Drax announced that it was abandoning plans to develop the gas-fired power station. The company said that it was committed to being carbon-negative by 2030.[5]

Transport Action Network

Another case filed shortly after the Heathrow ANPS decision was a legal challenge by the campaign group Transport Action Network (TAN). This group hoped to challenge the government's £27bn new roads infrastructure plan, Road Investment Strategy 2 (RIS2), announced in the budget in the early days of the COVID-19 pandemic. In the 'largest ever' road building announcement, it proposed to complete four thousand miles of new roads by 2025, including high-profile schemes such as a tunnel under Stonehenge and the long-mooted Oxford–Cambridge expressway. Transport has so far been one of the worst performing sectors in decarbonisation, today accounting for about 28% of the UK's CO2 emissions. This figure has barely changed since the 1990s while other sectors such as electricity generation have significantly decarbonised.

'The Heathrow judgment gave us confidence that challenges based on climate change would be taken seriously by the courts,' says Chris Todd, who previously worked at the Campaign for Better Transport and set up Transport Action Network in

2019.[6] The application for a judicial review was on the basis that the Department for Transport were using many existing plans for road expansion which had been drawn up before the Net Zero commitment was made in 2019 – TAN argued that in light of the new legal requirements and the Net Zero target, the RIS2 strategy should be reviewed. It also argued that the Secretary of State for Transport was obliged to take into account a quantitative assessment of how the increased carbon emissions from the projects would impact on the achievement of key objectives in the UK. This assessment should include the Paris Agreement's provisions on rapid reductions in green-house gases, the Net Zero target for the UK in 2050 and the fourth and fifth carbon budgets under CCA 08.

TAN was represented by Leigh Day solicitors, and the case was argued in court by David Wolfe and Pete Lockley. In pre-trial hearings the DfT argued that the carbon implications of the project would be managed using the upcoming Transport Decarbonisation Plan. This strategy was expected to recommend the expedition of electric vehicles, with the assumption that even if more cars end up on the road, the fleet's overall carbon footprint would reduce. During the JR hearings, the transport minister Grant Shapps claimed that the additional emissions from the plan would only amount to $0.27MtCO2e$, meaning that they would be so small that no review was needed. However, the court also heard from two expert witnesses who said that the expected emissions from RIS 2 could actually be 100 times higher than that. The discrepancy appears to be attributable to accounting differences; carbon construction emissions were expected to be included in emissions trading schemes and therefore left out of account, the plan assessed only the new schemes announced (instead of including the existing plans) and assumptions were made that electric vehicles would quickly replace all existing diesel and petrol vehicles and therefore emissions overall would fall.[7]

In July 2020 TAN was given permission to proceed with the JR on climate grounds by Mrs Justice Lieven, who declared the case to be 'significant' which meant it should be fast-tracked. In December 2020, TAN launched a second case, arguing that the NPS for National Networks should be reviewed, reflecting the Heathrow JR and the ENPS case. This document, setting out planning policy for new roads (and rail), was published in 2014, again before the Paris Agreement was signed and before the Net Zero commitment had been made in 2019. Official correspondence released as part of the case showed that DfT officials had advised the transport secretary Grant Shapps to review the NPS based on the new Net Zero commitments, but that he had overridden that advice.[8]

TAN again worked with Leigh Day and David Wolfe. 'What really gave us impetus was the commitment to Net Zero in 2019,' says Chris Todd. 'Given that the target changed from 80% to Net Zero we couldn't afford any increase in emissions from transport such as from an expanded road network increasing traffic and new car-dependent housing. It showed we couldn't just keep putting off responsibility for the huge changes we need to make.'[9]

In July 2021 TAN lost the first RIS 2 case. Mr Justice Holgate judged that DfT officials had given Shapps 'laconic' advice that the road-building programme was consistent with Net Zero targets. His judgment found that the claimants had not been able to show that the decision to proceed with RIS 2 was 'irrational' or in 'bad faith', the tests for a JR to succeed. The judge added that the transport secretary did not need to know the precise numbers in order to decide whether the project would actually jeopardise decarbonisation targets or not. Chris Todd told *The Guardian* that he was 'shocked'. However, the second JR had more success – the DfT announced in July 2021 that the Roads NPS would be reviewed, although refused to suspend it in the meantime.

Another case was *Elliot Smith v Department for Business, Energy and Industrial Strategy*. This case was heard in April 2021, and was again worked on by Rowan Smith from Leigh Day solicitors and David Wolfe QC. The claimant argued that in deciding not to include waste incinerators in the newly launched UK Emissions Trading Scheme (which replaced the EU ETS from January 2021), the Secretary of State at BEIS had failed to have regard to the Paris Agreement. While the case failed at the High Court, it was a point of law that the Paris Agreement was a relevant consideration for domestic decisions that affect the climate.

Yet another case was filed by veteran broadcaster Chris Packham. Represented by David Wolfe, Packham requested a judicial review of the decision to proceed with the works on the HS2 railway. The case argued that the Oakervee review into whether HS2 should proceed did not give the Secretary of State for Transport enough information to make an informed decision on the project. Among several grounds including damage to wildlife habitats, Packham also argued that the use of concrete in the construction phase of HS2 would cause 8–14 $MtCO_2e$ to be emitted, contravening Britain's legal obligations to reduce its emissions under the Paris Agreement. However, his appeal against the judge's refusal of an application for JR was rejected in July 2020.

Good Law Project and Heathrow

The Good Law Project also decided to try to further the gains made in the Court of Appeal judgment in the Heathrow case. In December 2020, three days after the Supreme Court judgment came in, the GLP was back with another threat of legal proceedings. This time the legal campaign group focused on the changing circumstances and scientific understanding of the impacts of climate change. The Supreme Court judgment had reaffirmed that the climate impact of the third runway would be assessed against current targets at the DCO stage, the Net Zero target. GLP requested a new JR reviewing the targets of the original ANPS in the light of the new Net Zero commitments. Again supported by Dale Vince and George Monbiot, the request aimed to replicate the success of the request to review the ENPS (see above), and tried to rectify what Cait Hewitt from AEF had called the 'ultimate policy approval' for Heathrow expansion. In challenging the fact that the reinstated ANPS still relied on the old 80% target from CCA 08, the GLP challenge tried to show how important these national policy statements are in setting the overall tone for climate-friendly development. The case received support from barrister Alex Goodman, who had argued the ENPS case for GLP, and QC Phillippa Kaufmann.

The claim argued that the ANPS should be reviewed in the light of the government's Net Zero commitment in 2019. It was a very similar approach to the request to review the ENPS under section 6 Planning Act 2008 when there has been a significant change in the landscape surrounding the policy. This approach had succeeded just a few months previously when the BEIS secretary had agreed to review the ENPS policy statement. Convincing the government to review an NPS is generally viewed as a high bar, unless the policy is very old and out of date. Alex Goodman says that the passing of the Carbon Budget Order in 2021, which establishes the legal framework for the sixth carbon budget and reflects the Net Zero commitment, may now prove to be key. As this is domestic law it avoids the question of the applicability of the Paris Agreement in UK law, and has the stamp of Parliamentary approval. 'This promise of a 78% reduction by 2035 is so much faster than anything we've seen before,' says Goodman. 'We have the commitment to include IAS and now there are only thirteen years left. We hope that a court will see how urgent this is.'[10]

In late 2021 GLP sent another letter to the government, again requesting a review of the ANPS. The government responded that it would promise to consider a review of the NPS once its Jet Zero strategy is finalised (expected 2022). GLP decided that the court would be likely to offer the government time to finalise the strategy and has postponed issuing a pre-trial action letter in which it would ask the government to reappraise the carbon impacts and the economic benefits of the third runway project.

Manston Airport

There was no respite for the beleaguered ANPS. In February 2021 another momentous decision dragged the controversial document back into the spotlight. The Secretary of State for Transport approved the first ever airports DCO under the NPS, for the redevelopment of Manston Airport in Kent. Developers RiverOak were given the go-ahead to develop the former Battle of Britain airfield near the Thanet coast into a multi-million-pound cargo hub. Campaigners argued that the development would be highly polluting, using some of the heaviest and dirtiest cargo planes, and would impact on congestion and the UK's ability to meet its carbon budgets. A two-year review by four planning inspectors under the DCO rules concluded that the airport would have 'a material impact on the ability of the government to meet its carbon targets', including international commitments,[11] and recommended against the granting of development consent. Nevertheless, the DCO was approved by Grant Shapps. Campaigner Jennifer Dawes launched a crowd-funder which raised over £90,000 to cover the costs of instructing a QC and Harrison Grant solicitors to take on the case. In his judgment at the High Court, Mr Justice Holgate ruled that there were failings in the way the original decision to grant a DCO had been made. He required the decision to be retaken and asked the Secretary of State to explain the reasons for his decision in more detail. The victory was significant because it is the first time since the Planning Act was passed in 2008 that a DCO for a Nationally Significant Infrastructure Project has been successfully challenged and overthrown. Climate and emissions-reduction arguments were front and centre in the JR claim.

The impact of the Heathrow JR

When the Court of Appeal ruled in favour of the climate claimants in the Heathrow JR in February 2020, the judgment was reported around the world. Social media was ablaze with the idea it could represent the UK's *Urgenda* moment, a reference to a case in the Netherlands where a court had ruled that the Dutch government must reduce emissions immediately in line with its human rights obligations. The Heathrow judgment seemed to show that countries could no longer continue to develop business-as-usual, high-carbon projects in the Net Zero world, and provided a 'beacon of hope' for activists.[12] As all the cases outlined in this chapter have shown, there is much left to play for. Even though the Heathrow JR did eventually fail, it exposed in a dramatic way the many fault-lines in the UK's current approach to bringing infrastructure development into line with the commitments made in Paris in 2015. Arguments are being tested and refined across a whole host of solicitors' firms and barristers' chambers. It seems clear that more challenges will follow. 'Courts are a serious way to put pressure to show that the government sticks to what it promised,' says Joana Setzer. 'All these cases are trying to make governments accountable for what they promised. They show that citizens are tired of broken promises.'[13]

However, the parallels between Heathrow and *Urgenda* may have been stretched too far. In that case, the Dutch Supreme Court decided after (six) years and several appeals on both sides that the Netherlands' overall emissions mitigation targets were insufficient. The case (a contraction of 'Urgent Agenda'), the culmination of a social movement involving 800 different groups calling for better climate targets, confirmed finally and definitively that 'Dutch climate change policy did not fulfil the state's duty of care *vis-à-vis* the public in a way that safeguards human rights'.[14] The ruling ordered the Dutch state to increase its ambition on climate mitigation and pursue a GHG-emissions reduction target of at least 25% by the end of 2020, instead of the pledged 19%.

While *Urgenda* was an attempt to bring an entire economy along with Net Zero, the Heathrow JR was just one case about one runway. It was an impactful piece of what is known as 'project-based litigation', but as Veerle Heyvaert from London School of Economics argues, it was 'by no stretch of the imagination an activist judgment'.[15] On procedural grounds, it was not a very sexy win. As we have seen, all of the legal challenges against the ANPS have so far failed to achieve an overhaul of the established national policy on airport expansion, a higher goal. Furthermore, because the CCA 08 was so progressive in setting targets, it remains difficult to challenge overall emissions reduction targets, as happened in *Urgenda*. The Plan B Earth JR on the CCA 08 emissions reduction targets from 2018 showed that a challenge to the adequacy of the CCA 08 targets was likely to be unsuccessful.

Yet legal targets can only achieve so much without public pressure and policy action to ensure that they are met. In this respect we can see that the symbolic impact of the Heathrow JR has emerged as its most important legacy. The case fell at a crucial time for the UK, in the middle of heated public arguments and mass protests demanding climate action. The High Court judgment affirming the decision to approve a new, high-carbon runway fell on the same day that Parliament declared a climate emergency. This case showed that even with the UK's strong climate law, the government still seemed to think that building an enormous third runway, promising an additional quarter of a million flights a year, could be acceptable.

The twists and turns of the Heathrow JR played out as climate policy was dramatically overhauled. By the time the Supreme Court verdict in the Heathrow case was announced in late 2020, the 80% emissions reduction target was consigned to history and Net Zero had become law. The Supreme Court judgment seems out of step to some observers in this new policy landscape. For the campaigners, this was part of the strategy. The legal case caused another delay to the Heathrow expansion plans and the work on the third runway has not yet begun. If key milestones on the road to achieving the requirements of the fifth and sixth carbon budgets are missed over the next few years, the scale of the emissions reductions needed across the entire economy will grow. It may prove even harder to demonstrate that expanding the airport will not jeopardise these legal requirements.

In addition, media coverage of the case during this period provoked many people, including me, to question how all of these most important decisions about the carbon impacts of major infrastructure developments are being made. Although the legal challenge was fiendishly complex, the contradiction in the decision to expand one of the world's busiest airports in the middle of climate breakdown was simple to understand. 'Litigation forces an issue into the limelight. It forces ordinary people who may have never thought about it to take a position. In this case the Friends of the Earth and Plan B arguments were intuitively correct for a lot of people,' argues Leo Murray, a former Plane Stupid activist.[16]

Now that the target is Net Zero, it seems unlikely that any new legal challenge argued specifically on the need to consider the Paris Agreement will succeed. According to James Maurici, QC for the government in the Heathrow JR, the viability of the legal argument that NPSs should reflect the Paris temperature limit has 'fallen victim to chronology'. By this he means the argument has been superseded by a significant update in the policy and legal framework – Net Zero – which reflects the requirements of the Paris Agreement. He argues that there is now a 'retreat' from this argument, evidenced in the decision in the Packham case. Maurici himself thinks there is still an opportunity to run legal challenges on aspects of the Paris Agreement other than the temperature arguments, such as the document's provisions on the need to act with urgency. However, any more challenges based on the temperature arguments will share the same fate; 'anyone who is considering trying this again, good luck to them'.[17]

The future of strategic climate litigation

As we have seen throughout this book many lawyers and campaigning law firms are looking to launch cases which seek to hold the government to account for delivering on targets to reduce emissions and tackle climate change. We have seen that challenging an individual infrastructure project's contribution to national GHG emissions and impact on the carbon budget – 'project-based litigation' – seems to be a lucrative vein to mine. The proposition that an expanded Heathrow would materially impact the UK's emissions reductions targets and the importance of the Paris Agreement 1.5°C temperature limit has been explored in court and through exchanges with the Climate Change Committee. Further work has been done in subsequent cases such as the GLP Heathrow case. Controversial plans to open a new coal mine in Cumbria were put on hold in March 2021 when the Secretary of State announced he would be calling in the planning application. This was in response to the threat of legal action from a campaign group, which argued that the annual emissions from the mine would exceed the total emissions budget for the entire coal-mining sector in the CCC's sixth carbon budget.

In the UK at least, where legal avenues to challenge government decisions are limited to judicial review, we can expect that there will be more cases of this kind. We may see more JRs being launched into how the climate impacts of major infrastructure projects are assessed at the stage of applying for a DCO, possibly overturning applications which have been granted. The UK's experience is unusual in that we already have a strong piece of legislation – the CCA 08 – and we are unlikely to see a challenge on the strength of these targets. Nevertheless, the CCA's future focus has its critics. The UK is still a few years away from a critical decision point about whether we will meet the fifth and sixth carbon budgets, and if we fail to reach these milestones it may be too late to act. 'As we get closer to these dates, and we get increasingly desperate for solutions, there may be more challenges on the adequacy of these budgets and how they are enforced,' argues Alex Goodman.[18] We may also see cases challenging on corporate greenwash – companies claiming to decarbonise while hiding behind offsetting. Another prominent case currently in the courts was launched under the Companies Act 2006: two university lecturers are calling on the Universities Superannuation Scheme to divest from fossil fuels.

Elsewhere in the world we are beginning to see an explosion in new ways of working. The Grantham Institute in conjunction with the Sabin Centre runs a database 'Climate change laws of the world' and currently counts a total of 1,846 litigation cases which 'raise issues of law or fact regarding the science of climate change and/or climate change mitigation and adaptation policies or efforts before an administrative, judicial or other investigatory body'.[19] It is clearly one of the hottest areas of climate action. Developments in other countries show what can be possible in other jurisdictions, such as the 2021 *Milieudefensie* case in the Netherlands which established that the oil giant Shell has a duty of care to Dutch residents to reduce its CO2 emissions. The ruling ordered the company to reduce its emissions by 45% by 2030. Legal analysts believe there may be an increase in the number of cases which invoke principles of the violation of human and constitutional rights, and especially issues of inter-generational rights. This has already been seen in the 2021 ruling in *The People v Arctic Oil* in Norway and the *Neubauer* case in Germany, both of which were led by young people. In the *Arctic Oil* case, a group of young people took the Norwegian government to the European Court of Human Rights, arguing that the country's oil drilling is harming young people's future; and in the German case the country's supreme constitutional court ruled in 2021 that emissions reduction provisions in Germany's main climate protection law were insufficient and this threatened the rights of future generations.

However, one big question still remains. Do any of these cases actually lead to a reduction in climate-wrecking emissions, the only thing which will help us meet our obligations under carbon budgets and ultimately to stop climate change? As the Paris Agreement reminds us, without rapid decarbonisation by 2030 the situation is bleak. Even as we hurtle towards that 1.5°C threshold, we have already seen ample evidence that climate change is affecting all of our lives today. Enforcement of the rulings in these legal cases may become the main battle ground of the future.

Harro van Asselt, Professor of Climate Law and Policy at the University of Eastern Finland, says it is very challenging to assess the overall impact of all these legal cases: 'What metric are we measuring against – did it lead to new laws? Did we stall a project, or is it just about building new social norms? Even in the most famous of these cases, the Dutch *Urgenda* case, we can't be sure that it even led to the emission reductions occurring.'[20]

The government review of JR

All of these cases were held against the backdrop of an ongoing government review into the JR process. The Conservative party committed to review the 'abuse' of judicial review in its election manifesto in 2019, seeming motivated by irritation at the apparent barrage of legal challenges, on climate, environment and other important aspects of government decision making. In July 2020 Lord Faulks QC was chosen to head up a panel of six judges hand-picked by the government to launch an investigation to 'ensure that Judicial Review is available to protect the rights of the individual against an overbearing state, while ensuring that it is not abused to conduct politics by another means or to create needless delays'.[21]

The manifesto commitment was widely interpreted as responding to two stinging Supreme Court judgments which upheld JRs launched by the campaigner Gina Miller. The first of these, in 2017, found that the government had erred in its judgement that Parliament did not need to be given a vote on whether to trigger Article 50 on leaving the European Union. The original verdict in the High Court in 2016 provoked a controversial 'enemies of the people' headline in the *Daily Mail*. The second, in September 2019, found that Boris Johnson's request to the Queen that Parliament be prorogued for five weeks at the height of the Brexit crisis was unlawful. At the time critics called this judgment a 'constitutional coup'.[22] Since the Supreme Court's first case was heard in 2009 it has seemed at pains to demonstrate its independence from government, and observers have argued that this is partly because previously its functions were carried out in the House of Lords. Critics have argued that this is why it ruled against the government in the Brexit case, but of course critics of the Heathrow judgment had argued the opposite – that the Supreme Court was determined to preserve the status quo.

Judicial review can be seen as troublesome to administrations precisely because it is designed to challenge government decisions, but as we have seen this is a limited power. The judges in the High Court and the Court of Appeal were at pains to point out that they were in no way passing judgment on the merits of Heathrow expansion, or whether any airport expansion was indeed compatible with what the government had committed to in the 2008 Climate Change Act. Their judgments merely reflected their assessment of whether the decision-making processes laid out in the 2008 Planning Act were correctly followed. None of the cases outlined above was capable of answering overarching questions of whether the UK's climate legislation is fit for purpose. As to whether emissions reductions are adequately targeted, or actually being made, it is only in the next ten years or so that we will see whether the UK is on track to meet the sixth carbon budget.

The lack of legal instruments available to lawyers wishing to challenge the government on climate change is due to specific features of the UK's unwritten constitution and its tradition of Parliamentary sovereignty. Courts are not able to overturn legislation made by Parliament, nor do they have the ability to review the way in which public bodies exercise the powers that Parliament has conferred on them.[23]

The Faulks review was published in March 2021. Broadly, it asserts the importance of JR, calling it an 'essential ingredient' of the rule of law, and recommends against any 'far-reaching' legislation in the area. The panel also found evidence that the number of claims are in fact decreasing and no suggestion that large numbers of claims lacking merit are being allowed to proceed. Legal opinion broadly interpreted the report to mean that no change is necessary in the provisions for JR. However, the day after the review was published, the Lord Chancellor Robert Buckland launched a public consultation into a number of reforms which would be designed to 'restore trust in the judicial review process', which seems a thinly veiled attempt to delineate which issues the courts can rule on and which they cannot.[24]

Senior judges, including retired Lord Robert Carnwath, have warned the government against challenging the independence of the judiciary, but the battle continues. In October 2021, the new justice secretary Dominic Raab unveiled plans in a Judicial Review and Courts Bill going through Parliament to further restrict JR, which he argued was being 'used to harpoon major infrastructure projects like the construction of new roads'.[25] Media reported that the prime minister's office was pushing for new rules which would allow ministers to ignore rulings from JRs that they disagree with.

CONCLUSION: WILL THERE BE A THIRD RUNWAY AT HEATHROW?

The UK should be rightly proud of its pioneering CCA 08 and the Act's innovative instrument, five-year carbon budgets for each economic sector. This law was achieved during a gloomy period in global climate negotiations as the concept of national commitments to emissions reduction targets under the Kyoto Protocol slowly unravelled. Recent commitments to Net Zero by 2050 and a 78% reduction in greenhouse gas emissions by 2035 are significantly more ambitious than the 2008 targets. The UK is one of the first countries to say it will go this far. In late 2021, it hosted the CoP26 climate change talks in Glasgow, a year after they were postponed due to the coronavirus pandemic. Prime minister Johnson was keen to showcase the UK's climate leadership on a global stage. Britain made important pledges to provide finance on things like forest protection, but a global agreement to increase ambition to limit temperature rises to 1.5°C seemed to be slipping out of reach. New national pledges would lead to a world of 2.4°C warming, according to Climate Action Tracker.[1] The CoP decision saw countries pledging to end coal-fired power and to phase out international finance for fossil fuels, but poorer countries baulked at the failure (again) to deliver the annual $100bn of adaptation funding promised by Obama in 2009 at Copenhagen.

The story of the Heathrow JR is essentially one of accountability. It is about finding ways to ensure that governments keep the ambitious promises they make in the spotlight at international conferences. The story has shown the tortuous and complex path a lawyer must follow to understand the nuts and bolts of how these loud proclamations on climate are supposed to become a reality. Many important arguments have been made about the economic importance of aviation and the role Heathrow plays in our global competitiveness, yet expanding Heathrow Airport in a climate emergency just *feels* wrong. Even so, there is a huge step between instinctively feeling that something is wrong and being able to quantify and challenge that effectively in a court of law. It comes down to painstaking trawling through frankly boring documents, an encyclopaedic knowledge of planning law, money, time and a lot of risk-taking. This case clearly shows the value in going back to the original planning documents to understand how the decisions on projects of this magnitude are made. Even though ultimately the case failed, it has shown that a group of dedicated, passionate lawyers can find gaps and failures in argument and expose the tensions between a business-as-usual economic system and the extremely challenging climate commitments we have been promised. Although the campaigners did not achieve a definitive end to the prospect of a third runway eventually being built, the JR process has helped to give the Paris Agreement 'tangibility' in UK law. It is this wider narrative which will be remembered.

Without this case, many people may have assumed that there was a workable solution to develop a third runway at

Will there be a third runway at Heathrow?

Heathrow and still keep GHG emissions under the 1.5°C limit. I hope this book has established that I believe the maths for mitigating the climate impacts of a proposed third runway still does not add up. There is still no real plan to mitigate the obviously increased CO2 emissions that a projected 260,000 extra flights a year will generate beyond an optimistic rehash of techno-optimism and reliance on offsetting and carbon pricing set out in documents such as the SA UK roadmap and the Aviation Decarbonisation Strategy. It will probably be an expensive drain on the UK economy. The detailed digging and analysis carried out by the lawyers and the courts throughout the JR process has exposed the inconsistencies in the whole approach.

When I first discussed this story with Will Rundle from FoE in the run-up to the High Court hearing, he said to me that the mitigation efforts in the Heathrow expansion plans would rely on largely unproven technologies. I remember thinking, yes but surely, if there has been an official government consultation and policy process, someone somewhere has done the sums and can explain how the third runway will not exceed the carbon budget. I went back to the original documents and spent months poring over the graphs, economic language and footnotes, convinced that there must be an explanation somewhere, that there must be something that everyone had missed. More than a year later I feel confident that there really isn't much to be missed.

If the GLP challenge succeeds in persuading the courts of the need to review the ANPS under the new Net Zero regime, along with the government's acceptance that emissions from international flights must now be included in carbon budgets, it will be a very tall order for Heathrow Airport to reconcile the inevitable increase in carbon emissions from more flights with the stringent requirements to reduce emissions. We have some indication of how they will attempt to square that circle in the consultation documents and the SA UK roadmap. Whether a DCO is granted or not, the way that Heathrow Airport quantifies those effects should be publicly available. We will see whether the government agrees with their confidence that offsetting, carbon pricing, SAF, 'efficiencies', technological leaps and all the other promises made by the Jet Zero partnership are enough to be sure that in thirty years' time the whole of UK aviation emits less than 23MtCO2e. And if the accounting looks dodgy or questionable, no doubt another JR will be launched into how the decision to grant the DCO was made.

Moreover, the economic case for the project continues to shift. When the ANPS was designated in 2018, there was an unquestioning acceptance that global demand for aviation is insatiable and that 70% growth in passenger numbers by 2050 would in effect be quite moderate. The Airports Commission final report showed that much of the rationale behind the recommendation for new runway capacity in the south-east was an assumption that current capacity was close to being stretched to the limit: 'with no availability at its main hub airport London is beginning to find that new routes to important long-haul destinations are set up elsewhere in Europe rather than in the UK'. Only one scenario in that report modelled what might happen if passenger demand actually reduced in the future, and this 'global fragmentation' scenario was only granted a few sentences in the final report.

But of course, as the Heathrow JR was winding its tortuous path to conclusion, coronavirus was spreading all around the world. Most of this spread was fuelled by air travel in our hyperconnected world. Much has been written about how repeated waves of the disease were seeded in the UK as passengers travelled from all over the world, bringing in fresh variants ahead of quarantine rules. And coronavirus hit the aviation industry harder than most. When the virus first took hold in March 2020, air passenger numbers collapsed almost overnight as all global airlines drastically reduced flights. In early 2021, IATA figures showed that demand was 75% lower in 2020 than in 2019. Heathrow was heavily affected. Within weeks airline companies had been given access to the Bank of England's generous COVID corporate financing facility which promised cheap loans to help companies stay afloat during the crisis; even while some companies (for example, easyJet) continued to pay dividends out to shareholders. Greenpeace and others called for these bailouts to have green strings attached, effectively granting the loans in return for commitments to decarbonise aviation.

Two years later, passenger numbers have yet to return to pre-pandemic levels. Quarantine rules from red list countries, vaccine passports, travel bans and ever-changing guidelines and designations for individual countries continue to make flying abroad seem too problematic for those who cannot afford to lose money if a booked holiday cannot be taken. Meanwhile, many others have rediscovered the pleasures of holidaying in the UK. A survey by the University of Bristol in April 2021 found that 60% of respondents said they actually intended to fly less, rather than more, after being double-vaccinated against the virus; many cited fears about spreading new variants around the world.[2]

At the same time profound changes have occurred in the way business has been conducted during the pandemic. Video conferencing through programmes such as Microsoft Teams and Zoom went from niche optimism among technological early adopters to being rolled out in every mainstream business across the country in a matter of weeks. Zoom's share price increased six-fold in the first nine months of 2020. It seems just the start of the development of video-conferencing facilities and options for working in smarter ways with less travel. Deflated business travellers who had spent years drinking tepid coffee in beige airport lounges, mourning yet another failure to make it home in time for the school sports day, saw the scales fall from their eyes. Working from home became socially acceptable almost overnight. Companies realised that expensive office space could be sold off, small meetings and negotiations worked perfectly well on video conferencing and that enormous budgets for business-class travel and built-in jet-lag affecting productivity could be a thing of the past. Before the pandemic Heathrow stated that 33% of passengers in 2018 were business travellers. How could the models from 2015, which assumed unassailable demand growth, possibly be taken seriously now? In a sparkling irony, in early 2021 Sir Howard Davies, chair of the Airports Commission, the very man who had barely seemed to consider whether growth in passenger numbers was anything other than inevitable, said that the third runway was currently no longer needed: Heathrow 'would be delighted just to fill the two runways it's got,' he told LBC.[3]

While it looks unlikely that the government will go head-to-head with Heathrow by taking an unequivocal decision to cancel Heathrow expansion, the third runway plan may yet be quietly shelved. Sources close to the company claim that the team working on the expansion plans have been redeployed to other tasks. Heathrow cannot simply throw its shareholders' money into a hole in the ground if the demand for flights never recovers. In October 2021, eighteen months into the pandemic, Heathrow Airports' top shareholder Ferrovial said it would not provide the company with any more investment finance.[4] Ferrovial's position may have been influenced by the fact that activist investor Chris Hohn, who donated money to Extinction Rebellion, secretly bought a 4% share in the company in 2019.[5] And the carbon costs of the project are only mounting. As we get closer and closer to the point at which we can no longer postpone deciding how we reach a 78% reduction from 1990s emission levels by 2035, the carbon case will only erode the economic justifications further. A New Economics Foundation (NEF) report presented to the All-Party Parliamentary Group on Heathrow expansion in December 2021 stated that the carbon abatement cost of the project had doubled from £50bn to £100bn since 2018. This is because BEIS figures for the 'carbon value' (see Chapter 2) have risen to £241 per tonne of CO_2 in line with the Net Zero commitments, with the calculations recognising that only a limited available capacity for easy and cheap offsetting and removals is left now.[6] According to the NEF report, if airport expansion does occur across the UK, these carbon costs, presumably largely funded by the public purse, will amount to a 'colossal' subsidy of around £62bn to the aviation industry. Little of that cost is likely to be recouped in the form of taxes on flying and the aviation industry.

The government has a choice. As we have seen, we can create a plausible scenario in which Heathrow expansion is allowed within the remaining carbon budget and it will not affect our ability to meet our commitments to reduce emissions. But if we do this, at what cost to all the other sectors which do not get preferential treatment? And at what cost to future generations?

While this book certainly does not recommend that everyone should stop flying tomorrow, and recognises the importance of personal contact in business and visiting relatives and friends around the world, it aims to question the assumptions underlying the need for perpetual growth in the aviation industry. Is this for the benefit of anyone other than the shareholders of aviation businesses and the very richest? If 50% of the UK population does not regularly fly, do the frequent flyers really need 70% more flights? Even if the number of flights at Heathrow returns to pre-pandemic levels, would preventing expansion really restrict the choices of anyone but a privileged few?

Why does aviation appear to get a free ride and why is the industry not being pressured further to move towards meaningful decarbonisation? Many of the aviation campaigners I interviewed for this book are certain that Heathrow Airport and others have the government's ear. They argue that when someone from the aviation industry promises to increase the use of sustainable fuel or another technological 'solution' to the problem of aviation's failure to decarbonise, they are met with a sympathetic hearing. Amidst increasing criticism of the government's big talk and little action on climate, it is hard not to conclude that the current administration is betting on a technological fix which will obviate uncomfortable choices and the need to suggest that growth in the aviation industry should be restricted.

But one thing does look certain. If Heathrow Airport does eventually decide to apply for a DCO to build the north-west runway and it is approved, we can expect lawyers such as the

Will there be a third runway at Heathrow?

Friends of the Earth team and David Wolfe, Rowan Smith, Pete Lockley and Tim Crosland to dust off their wigs and fight it all the way.

Time is being called on empty promises. There is much left to play for.

ABBREVIATIONS

AEF	Aviation Environment Federation
ANPS	Airports National Policy Statement
AoS	appraisal of sustainability under the Planning Act 2008
BAA	British Airports Authority; later BAA plc
BECCS	bio energy with carbon capture and storage
BEIS	Department for Business, Energy and Industrial Strategy
CCA 08	(UK) Climate Change Act 2008
CCC	(UK) Climate Change Committee – formerly the Committee on Climate Change
CFC	chlorofluorocarbon (gases)
CoP	Conference of Parties
CORSIA	Carbon Offsetting and Reduction Scheme for International Aviation
CPRE	Campaign to Protect Rural England
DACCS	direct air carbon capture and storage
DCO	development consent order
DEFRA	Department for Environment Food & Rural Affairs

Abbreviations

DfT	Department for Transport
ENPS	Energy National Policy Statement
EU	ETS EU Emissions Trading Scheme
EV	electrically propelled vehicles
FoE	Friends of the Earth
GHG	greenhouse gas(es)
GtCO2e	the equivalent of [number] gigatonnes of CO2
HAC	High Ambition Coalition
HACAN	Heathrow Association for the Control of Aircraft Noise
IAS	international aviation and shipping
IATA	International Air Transport Association
ICAO	International Civil Aviation Organization
(I)NDC	(intended) nationally determined contribution
IPCC	Inter-governmental Panel on Climate Change
JR	(Heathrow) judicial review
MtCO2e	the equivalent of [number] megatonnes of CO2
NDC(s)	nationally determined contribution(s)
NGO	non-government organisation
NOx	collectively, nitrogen oxides
NPS	National Policy Statement
NPV	net present value
ppm	parts per million
RIS 2	Department for Transport's Road Investment Strategy 2
RSPB	Royal Society for the Protection of Birds
SAF	sustainable aviation fuel
SA UK	Sustainable Aviation UK
S-CGE	strategic computable general equilibrium (economic modelling)

Abbreviations

SEA	strategic environmental assessment under the Planning Act 2008
TAN	Transport Action Network
UNFCCC	United Nations Framework Convention on Climate Change
WWF	World Wide Fund for Nature
XR	Extinction Rebellion

NOTES

Introduction

1   Niko Kommenda, 'How your flight emits as much CO2 as many people do in a year', *The Guardian*, 19 July 2019, www.theguardian. com/environment/ng-interactive/2019/jul/19/carbon-calculator-how-taking-one-flight-emits-as-much-as-many-people-do-in-a-year (accessed 10 January 2022).
2   'Heathrow expansion: plan overview', www.heathrow.com/comp any/about-heathrow/expansion/plan-overview (accessed 10 January 2022).

Chapter 1

1   Maria Ivanova, 'Politics, economy and society', in Daniel Klein, Maria Pia Carazo, Meinhert Dueller et al. (eds), *The Paris Agreement on Climate Change: Analysis and Commentary* (Oxford: Oxford University Press, 2017), 19.
2   Benito Müller, 'Copenhagen 2009: failure of final wake-up call for our leaders?', Oxford Institute for Energy Studies EV49, February 2010, https://web.archive.org/web/20100401012701/http://www. oxfordenergy.org/pdfs/EV49.pdf (accessed 10 January 2022), 6.
3   'Harrabin's notes: after Copenhagen', BBC News, 21 December 2009, http://news.bbc.co.uk/1/hi/sci/tech/8423822.stm (accessed 10 January 2022).

Notes

4   Müller, 'Copenhagen 2009', 6.

5   Andrew Higham, 'Pre-2020 climate action and the emergent role of non-party stakeholders', in Klein et al. (eds), *The Paris Agreement on Climate Change*, 44.

6   Albert Bates, *The Paris Agreement* (Cambridge: Ecovillage Imprints, 2015), 214.

7   Karl Mathiesen and Fiona Harvey, 'Coalition breaks cover in Paris to push for binding and ambitious deal', *The Guardian*, 8 December 2015, www.theguardian.com/environment/2015/dec/08/coalition-paris-push-for-binding-ambitious-climate-change-deal (accessed 10 January 2022).

8   Lavanya Rajamani and Emmanuel Guerin, 'Central concepts and how they evolved', in Klein et al. (eds), *The Paris Agreement on Climate Change*, 75.

9   Robert Falkner, 'The Paris Agreement and the new logic of international climate politics', *International Affairs* 92 (2016): 1107–25.

10 Mike Childs and Neil Carter, 'Friends of the Earth as a policy entrepreneur, the Big Ask campaign', *Environmental Politics* 6 (2018): 994–1013.

11 Thomas Muinzer, *Climate and Energy Governance for the UK Low Carbon Transition: The Climate Change Act 2008* (London: Palgrave Pivot, 2019), 8.

12 Childs and Carter, 'Friends of the Earth as a policy entrepreneur'.

13 Author interview (in person), Glasgow, 6 November 2021.

14 Childs and Carter, 'Friends of the Earth as a policy entrepreneur'.

15 Currently DEFRA.

16 Simon Evans, 'Analysis: UK's emissions have fallen 29% over the past decade', *CarbonBrief*, 3 March 2020, www.carbonbrief.org/analysis-uks-co2-emissions-have-fallen-29-per-cent-over-the-past-decade (accessed 10 January 2022).

17 *R on the application of Neil Richard Spurrier v The Secretary of State for Transport, Heathrow Airport Limited and ors; R on the application of 5 London Boroughs, Greenpeace Limited and the Mayor of London v The Secretary of State for Transport, Heathrow Airport Limited and ors; R on the application of Friends of the Earth Limited v The Secretary of State for Transport, Heathrow Airport Limited and Arora Holdings Limited; R on the application of Plan B Earth Limited v The Secretary of State for Transport, Heathrow Airport Limited and Arora Holdings Limited* [2019] EWHC 1070 (Admin) ('Heathrow High Court judgment'), para. 22, www.judiciary.uk/wp-content/

uploads/2019/05/Heathrow-main-judgment-1.5.19.pdf (accessed 10 January 2022).

18 HM Government, *Planning for a Sustainable Future*, White Paper (Cm 7120) 2007, 42.

19 The Secretaries of State for Transport, Communities and Local Government, and BEIS are responsible for different aspects of 'sustainable development'.

20 Friends of the Earth, Briefing on Heathrow expansion, 28 May 2020.

21 In the Heathrow case, the Secretary of State for Transport.

22 Heathrow High Court judgment, para. 644.

23 'AEF climate change: the basics', Aviation Environment Federation (nd) www.aef.org.uk/what-we-do/climate/ (accessed 10 January 2022).

24 Peter McManners, *Fly and Be Damned* (London: Zed Books, 2012), 7.

25 Climate Change Committee, 'Sixth Carbon Budget', www.theccc.org.uk/publication/sixth-carbon-budget/ (accessed 7 February 2022), Aviation sector, 5.

26 Stefan Gössling and Andreas Humpe, 'The global scale, distribution and growth of aviation: implications for climate change', *Global Environmental Change* 65 (2020), https://doi.org/10.1016/j.gloenvcha.2020.102194.

27 Evans, 'Analysis: UK's emissions'.

28 McManners, *Fly and Be Damned*, 7.

29 J.E. Penner, D.H. Lister, D.J. Griggs, D.J. Dokken and M. McFarland (eds), *Aviation and the Global Atmosphere*, prepared in collaboration with the Scientific Assessment Panel to the Montreal Protocol on Substances that Deplete the Ozone Layer (Cambridge: Cambridge University Press, 1999).

30 David S. Lee, 'The current state of scientific understanding of the non-CO_2 effects of aviation on climate', Manchester Metropolitan University, report for Department of Transport, December 2018, https://assets.publishing.service.gov.uk/government/uploads/system/uploads/attachment_data/file/813342/non-CO_2-effects-report.pdf (accessed 10 January 2022).

31 *Ibid.*

32 D.S. Lee, D.W. Fahey, A. Skowron et al., 'The contribution of global aviation to anthropogenic climate forcing for 2000 to 2018', *Atmospheric Environment* 244 (2021), https://doi.org/10.1016/j.atmosenv.2020.117834.

Notes

33 Lee, 'Current scientific understanding of non-CO2 effects'.

34 Committee on Climate Change, 'Net Zero: The UK's contribution to stopping global warming', May 2019, www.theccc.org.uk/wp-content/uploads/2019/05/Net-Zero-The-UKs-contribution-to-stopping-global-warming.pdf (accessed 10 January 2022). The Committee is now called the Climate Change Committee.

35 CCC, 'Sixth Carbon Budget', Aviation sector summary.

36 McManners, *Fly and Be Damned*, 1.

37 Department for Transport, *Airports National Policy Statement: new runway capacity and infrastructure at airports in the South East of England* (London: OGL, 2018) (ANPS), section 1.1.

38 Aviation Environment Federation, 'The UK's Net Zero target: is aviation in or out?', 17 December 2019, www.aef.org.uk/2019/12/17/the-uks-net-zero-target-is-aviation-in-or-out/ (accessed 10 January 2022).

39 Hannah Ritchie, 'Climate change and flying: what share of global emissions come from aviation?', Our World in Data, 22 October 2020, https://ourworldindata.org/co2-emissions-from-aviation (accessed 10 January 2022).

40 Beatriz Martinez Romera, 'The Paris Agreement and the regulation of international bunker fuels', *Review of European, Comparative & International Environmental Law (RECIEL)* 25:2 (2016): 215–27, https://doi.org/10.1111/reel.12170.

41 'Analysis: aviation could consume a quarter of 1.5C budget by 2050', CarbonBrief, 8 August 2016, www.carbonbrief.org/aviation-consume-quarter-carbon-budget (accessed 10 January 2022).

42 'Corsia: The UN's plan to "offset" growth in aviation emissions', CarbonBrief, 4 February 2019, www.carbonbrief.org/corsia-un-plan-to-offset-growth-in-aviation-emissions-after-2020 (accessed 9 March 2022).

43 Jörgen Larsson, Anna Elofsson, Thomas Sterner and Jonas Åkerman, 'International and national climate policies: a review', *Climate Policy* 19 (2019): 787–99, https://doi.org/10.1080/14693062.2018.1562871.

44 *Ibid.*

45 European Commission, 'Reducing emissions from aviation', https://ec.europa.eu/clima/policies/transport/aviation_en (accessed 10 January 2022).

46 Lord Deben, letter to Grant Shapps, 24 September 2019.

Notes

Chapter 2

1 Bethan Bell, 'The villages living under Heathrow's death sentence', BBC News, 25 October 2016, www.bbc.co.uk/news/uk-england-37667371 (accessed 10 January 2022).

2 Heathrow Airport Ltd, 'Heathrow: our history', www.heathrow.com/company/about-heathrow/our-history (accessed 10 January 2022).

3 Heathrow Association for the Control of Aircraft Noise (HACAN), 'Flight paths at a glance', https://hacan.org.uk/?page_id=3311 (accessed 10 January 2022).

4 E. Mazareanu, 'Hub connectivity of international airports worldwide in 2019, by airport', *Statista*, June 2019, www.statista.com/statistics/1125365/global-hub-airports-connectivity/ (accessed 10 January 2022).

5 CAPA – Centre for Aviation, 'UK's international hub not Heathrow', 12 November 2019, https://centreforaviation.com/analysis/reports/uks-international-hub-airport-not-heathrow-amsterdam-still-main-hub-499826 (accessed 10 January 2022).

6 'Paris Charles de Gaulle overtakes Heathrow as Europe's busiest airport', *Airport Review*, 29 October 2020, www.internationalairportreview.com/news/142243/paris-charles-de-gaulle-overtakes-heathrow/ (accessed 10 January 2022).

7 Department for Transport, 'The future of air transport', December 2003, 7, https://assets.publishing.service.gov.uk/government/uploads/system/uploads/attachment_data/file/685595/6046.pdf (accessed 10 January 2022).

8 Owen Bowcott and agencies, 'Heathrow protestors win third runway court victory', *The Guardian*, 26 March 2010, www.theguardian.com/environment/2010/mar/26/heathrow-third-runway-travel-and-transport (accessed 10 January 2022).

9 John Stewart, *Victory Against All the Odds: The Story of How the Campaign to Stop a Third Runway at Heathrow was Won* (London: HACAN, 2010).

10 Simon Jenkins, 'London's airports and a string of broken promises', *Evening Standard*, 27 March 2012, www.standard.co.uk/comment/comment/london-s-airports-and-a-string-of-broken-promises-7592940.html (accessed 10 January 2022).

11 Airports Commission, 'Airports Commission: interim report', December 2013, 6, https://assets.publishing.service.gov.uk/government/uploads/

system/uploads/attachment_data/file/271231/airports-commission-interim-report.pdf (accessed 10 January 2022).

12 Airports Commission, 'Airports Commission: final report', July 2015, 11, https://assets.publishing.service.gov.uk/government/uploads/system/uploads/attachment_data/file/440316/airports-commission-final-report.pdf (accessed 10 January 2022).

13 Airports Commission, 'Consultation document: Gatwick Airport second runway, Heathrow Airport extended northern runway, Heathrow Airport north west runway', November 2014, p. 70, www.planetalking.co.uk/wp-content/uploads/2014/11/Airports-Commission-Consultation-Document.pdf (accessed 9 March 2022).

14 Simon Roach, 'Heathrow runway could leave 1.6m people with aircraft noise', *Unearthed*, 17 May 2019, https://unearthed.green peace.org/2019/05/17/heathrow-third-runway-noise-pollution-lon don/ (accessed 10 January 2022).

15 John Collingridge, 'Passengers face risk for Heathrow's new runway', *The Times*, 13 August 2017, www.thetimes.co.uk/article/passengers-face-risk-for-heathrows-new-runway-npg2xnqmn (accessed 10 January 2022).

16 'A note from expert advisors, Prof. Peter Mackie and Mr Brian Pearce, on key issues considering the Airports Commission economic case', 5 May 2015, https://assets.publishing.service.gov.uk/govern ment/uploads/system/uploads/attachment_data/file/438981/economy-expert-panelist-wider-economic-impacts-review.pdf (accessed 10 January 2022).

17 The Green Book is issued by the Treasury. It describes how the Treasury appraises 'policies, programmes and projects'.

18 Deloitte, 'Review of PwC analysis conducted for Airports Commission', 16 October 2015, www.gatwickairport.com/globalassets/publication files/business_and_community/all_public_publications/second_runway/gov_submissions/249-apdx-deloitte-report-review-of-pwc-analysis-by-ac-oct-2015.pdf (accessed 10 January 2022).

19 Louise Smith, 'Planning for nationally significant infrastructure projects', 17 July 2017, https://commonslibrary.parliament.uk/research-briefings/sn06881/ (accessed 10 January 2022).

20 House of Commons Transport Committee, 'Airport National Policy Statement: third report of session 2017–19', 23 March 2018, https://publications.parliament.uk/pa/cm201719/cmselect/cmtrans/548/548.pdf (accessed 10 January 2022).

21 ANPS, section 2.32.
22 Sandra Laville, 'Cleanup cost of Heathrow third runway doubles to £100bn, MPs told', *The Guardian*, 22 December 2021, www.theguardian. com/environment/2021/dec/22/cleanup-cost-of-heathrow-third-runway-doubles-to-100bn-mps-told (accessed 10 January 2022).
23 Interviewed by author (in person), December 2021.
24 ANPS, section 5.82.
25 'How can Heathrow add 50% more flights without impacting the UK's ability to meet climate targets?', AEF, 25 July 2019, www. aef.org.uk/2019/07/25/how-can-heathrow-add-50-more-flights-without-impacting-the-uks-ability-to-meet-carbon-targets/ (accessed 10 January 2022).
26 Air Expansion Consultation, 'Heathrow Airport expansion: consultation document', June 2019, 88, www.heathrow.com/content/dam/ heathrow/web/common/documents/company/about/consulta tion/airport expansion consultation.pdf (accessed 10 January 2022).
27 Committee on Climate Change, letter from Lord Deben to Chris Grayling, 14 June 2018.
28 *Ibid.*
29 Jonathan Leake and Caroline Wheeler, 'No. 10 "fixes" Heathrow vote', *The Sunday Times*, 24 June 2018, www.thetimes.co.uk/article/ no-10-fixes-heathrow-runway-vote-msjbw9fx6 (accessed 10 January 2022).

Chapter 3

1 Interviewed by author (Zoom), 5 July 2021.
2 *Ibid.*
3 Interviewed by author (in person), 18 May 2021.
4 *Ibid.*
5 'Plan B & 11 citizens v UK 2050 carbon target', https://planb.earth/ plan-b-v-uk/ (accessed 10 January 2022).
6 Phillip Paiement, 'Urgent agenda, how climate litigation builds trans-national narratives', *Transnational Legal Theory* 11 (2020): 121–43, https://doi.org/10.1080/20414005.2020.1772617.
7 Interviewed by author (Zoom), 7 December 2021.
8 Interviewed by author (phone), 19 October 2021.
9 Interviewed by author (Zoom), 20 April 2021.

10 Raphael Hogarth, 'Judicial review', Institute for Government, 9 March 2020, www.instituteforgovernment.org.uk/explainers/judicial-review (accessed 10 January 2022).

11 'Councils, Mayor of London and Greenpeace will ask court to quash Heathrow decision', Hillingdon Council, 11 March 2019, https://hillingdon.gov.uk/article/2101/Councils-Mayor-of-London-and-Greenpeace-will-ask-court-to-quash-Heathrow-decision (accessed 10 January 2022).

12 Interviewed by author (Zoom), 20 April 2021.

13 Interviewed by author (Zoom), 29 September 2021.

14 The interns who worked on this over two-and-a-half years include Sonam Gordhan, Gabriella de Souza Crook, Julia Eriksen, Consolata Enobakhare, Isabella Dennis and Alexandra Musset.

15 Interviewed by author (in person), 18 May 2021.

16 Interviewed by author (Zoom), 11 June 2021.

17 Interviewed by author (Zoom), 29 September 2021.

18 BEIS, 'The clean growth strategy: leading the way to a low carbon future', amended version, October 2017, https://assets.publishing.service.gov.uk/government/uploads/system/uploads/attachment_data/file/700496/clean-growth-strategy-correction-april-2018.pdf (accessed 10 January 2022).

19 Interviewed by author (Zoom), 23 February 2021.

20 Interviewed by author (Zoom), 29 September 2021.

21 Heathrow High Court judgment, para. 636.

22 Friends of the Earth, 'Briefing: Heathrow expansion – illegal', 27 February 2020, https://cdn.friendsoftheearth.uk/sites/default/files/downloads/Friends of the Earth Legal Briefing – Heathrow Judgment – 27 Feb 2020 final.pdf (accessed 10 January 2022).

23 Quoted in *R (Friends of the Earth Ltd and others) v Heathrow Airport Limited* [2020] UKSC 53 (Supreme Court judgment), para. 88.

24 Committee on Climate Change, 'UK climate action following the Paris Agreement', October 2016, 12, www.theccc.org.uk/wp-content/uploads/2016/10/UK-climate-action-following-the-Paris-Agreement-Committee-on-Climate-Change-October-2016.pdf (accessed 10 January 2022). The Committee is now called the Climate Change Committee.

25 Who resemble 'Swampy', the legend from the Newbury bypass protests of the 1990s.

26 IPCC, 'Summary for policymakers', 2018, 5, www.ipcc.ch/site/

assets/uploads/sites/2/2019/05/SR15_SPM_version_report_
LR.pdf (accessed 10 January 2022).

27 Email correspondence with author, 14 October 2021.

28 Heathrow High Court judgment, para. 219.

29 *Ibid.*, para. 631(iv).

30 Committee on Climate Change, 'Net Zero: the UK's contribution
to stopping global warming', May 2019, 10, www.theccc.org.uk/
wp-content/uploads/2019/05/Net-Zero-The-UKs-contribution-
to-stopping-global-warming.pdf (accessed 10 January 2022). The
Committee is now called the Climate Change Committee.

31 *Ibid.*, 12.

32 Interviewed by author (phone), 15 July 2021.

33 Committee on Climate Change, 'Net Zero', 206.

34 Lord Deben, letter to Grant Shapps, 24 September 2019.

35 Interviewed by author (Zoom), 29 September 2021.

36 Interviewed by author (in person), 22 September 2021.

37 Email correspondence with author, 14 October 2021.

38 Interviewed by author (Zoom), 5 July 2021.

39 Quoted in Damian Carrington, 'Heathrow third runway ruled illegal over climate change', *The Guardian*, 27 February 2020, www.
theguardian.com/environment/2020/feb/27/heathrow-third-
runway-ruled-illegal-over-climate-change (accessed 10 January 2021).

40 *R (on application of Friends of the Earth) v Department for Transport & Others*
[2019] EWHC 1070 (Admin) (Appeal court judgment), 27 February
2020 www.judiciary.uk/wp-content/uploads/2020/02/Heathrow-
judgment-on-planning-issues-27-February-2020.pdf (accessed 11
March 2021), para. 234(2).

41 Hogarth, 'Judicial review'.

42 Appeal court judgment, para. 258.

43 Email correspondence with author, 14 October 2021.

44 Appeal court judgment, para. 277.

45 Friends of the Earth, 'Heathrow airport expansion – Supreme Court
Appeal briefing', 5 October 2020, https://friendsoftheearth.uk/
climate/heathrow-airport-expansion-supreme-court-appeal-briefing
(accessed 10 January 2022).

46 Both statements in Grantham Institute, 'Global trends in climate
litigation: lessons for CoP26 – video', 2 July 2021, www.lse.ac.uk/
granthaminstitute/events/global-trends-in-climate-litigation-lessons-
for-cop26/ (accessed 10 January 2022).

47 Interviewed by author (in person), 18 May 2021.

48 Carrington, 'Heathrow third runway ruled illegal'.

49 Dominic Casciani, 'What is the UK Supreme Court?', BBC News, 13 January 2020, www.bbc.co.uk/news/uk-49663001 (accessed 10 January 2022).

50 Interviewed by author (Zoom), 23 February 2021.

51 *Ibid.*

52 Interviewed by author (Zoom), 11 November 2021.

53 CCC, 'Sixth Carbon Budget', Aviation sector summary.

54 'CCC: UK must cut emissions "78% by 2035" to be on course for net-zero goal', *CarbonBrief*, 9 December 2020, www.carbonbrief.org/ccc-uk-must-cut-emissions-78-by-2035-to-be-on-course-for-net-zero-goal (accessed 10 January 2022).

55 Supreme Court judgement, para. 112.

56 Damian Carrington, 'Top UK court overturns block on Heathrow's third runway', *The Guardian*, 10 January 2022, www.theguardian.com/environment/2020/dec/16/top-uk-court-overturns-block-on-heathrows-third-runway (accessed 10 January 2022).

57 Interviewed by author (phone), January 2021.

58 Friends of the Earth, 'Briefing: Heathrow expansion – Supreme Court judgment', 16 December 2020, https://cdn.friendsoftheearth.uk/sites/default/files/downloads/HEATHROW_SUPREME_COURT_BRIEFING_DEC2020.pdf (accessed 9 March 2022).

59 Interviewed by author (in person), 26 May 2021.

60 *In the matter of Her Majesty's Attorney General v Crosland* [2021] UKSC 58, opening submission, 10 May 2021.

61 FoE, 'Briefing: Heathrow expansion'.

62 Interviewed by author (Zoom), 7 December 2021.

63 Interviewed by author (Zoom), 5 July 2021.

64 *Ibid.*

Chapter 4

1 IATA, 'Climate change', https://iata.org.xy2401.com/policy/environment/Pages/climate-change.aspx.html (accessed 9 March 2022).

2 European Commission, 'EU Emissions Trading System (EU ETS)', https://ec.europa.eu/clima/policies/ets_en (accessed 10 January 2022).

3   Silke Goldberg and Jannis Bille, 'The UK ETS after Brexit', Herbert Smith Freehills LLP, 11 March 2021, https://bit.ly/3r1lWNP (accessed 10 January 2022).

4   Ruth Wright, 'Wizz Air CEO calls carbon offsetting "a bit of a joke" yet offers it to customers', *euronews.green*, 11 October 2021, www.euronews.com/green/2021/10/11/wizz-air-ceo-calls-carbon-offsetting-a-bit-of-a-joke-yet-offers-it-to-customers (accessed 10 January 2022).

5   Andrew Murphy, '85% of offsets failed to reduce emissions, says EU study', *Transport & Environment*, 17 May 2017, www.transportenvironment.org/discover/85-offsets-failed-reduce-emissions-says-eu-study/ (accessed 10 January 2022).

6   AEF, 'Why Heathrow can't solve its carbon problem', March 2019, www.aef.org.uk/uploads/2019/03/Why-Heathrow-can't-solve-its-carbon-problem-.pdf (accessed 10 January 2022).

7   Geert de Cock, 'How to ensure the sustainability of electrofuels', *Transport & Environment*, 19 January 2021, www.transportenvironment.org/discover/how-ensure-sustainability-electrofuels/ (accessed 10 January 2022).

8   European Union Aviation Safety Agency, 'Sustainable aviation fuels', www.easa.europa.eu/eaer/climate-change/sustainable-aviation-fuels (accessed 10 January 2022).

9   Transport and Environment, 'Getting it right from the start: How to ensure the sustainability of electrofuels', January 2021, www.transportenvironment.org/wp-content/uploads/2021/07/T&E%20Briefing%20sustainability%20RFNBOs_202101.pdf (accessed 9 March 2022).

10   CCC, 'Sixth Carbon Budget', Aviation sector summary.

11   Alex Daniel, 'Electric-powered regional flights "could be taking off by 2030"', *City AM*, 24 September 2019, www.cityam.com/electric-powered-regional-flights-could-be-taking-off-by-2030/ (accessed 10 January 2022).

12   Alex Daniel, 'British Airways boss says electric planes idea won't fly until 2050', *City AM*, 17 October 2019, www.cityam.com/british-airways-boss-limited-opportunity-for-electric-planes-until-2050/ (accessed 10 January 2022).

13   Sustainable Aviation, 'Decarbonisation road-map: a path to Net Zero', www.sustainableaviation.co.uk/wp-content/uploads/2020/02/

SustainableAviation_CarbonLeaflet_20200129.pdf(accessed 10 January 2022).

14　*Ibid.*

15　Gwyn Topham, 'Can the aviation industry really go carbon neutral by 2050?', *The Guardian*, 7 February 2020, www.theguardian.com/business/2020/feb/07/can-the-aviation-industry-really-go-carbon-neutral-by-2050 (accessed 10 January 2022).

16　Heathrow Airport, 'Heathrow 2.0: carbon neutral growth roadmap', www.heathrow.com/content/dam/heathrow/web/common/documents/company/heathrow-2-0-sustainability/futher-reading/Carbon-Neutral-Growth-Roadmap.pdf (accessed 10 January 2022).

17　AEF, 'Why Heathrow can't solve its carbon problem'.

18　Heathrow Airport, 'Emissions strategy and action plan', May 2018, www.heathrow.com/content/dam/heathrow/web/common/documents/company/heathrow-2-0-sustainability/futher-reading/heathrow-emissions-strategy.pdf (accessed 10 January 2022).

19　AEF, 'Why Heathrow can't solve its carbon problem'.

20　Air Expansion Consultation, 'Heathrow expansion: consultation document', p. 88.

21　Jon Stone, 'UK government claims people must keep flying to cut carbon emissions', *The Independent*, 15 September 2021, www.independent.co.uk/climate-change/news/cop26-carbon-emissions-flying-net-zero-aviation-uk-b1920556.html (accessed 10 January 2022).

22　Stefan Gössling and Andreas Humpe, 'The global scale, distribution and growth of aviation: implications for climate change', *Global Environmental Change* 65 (2020), https://doi.org/10.1016/j.gloenvcha.2020.102194.

23　'Government puts up, then almost instantly withdraws, document showing need for behaviour change to cut carbon emissions', Airport Watch, 21 October 2021, www.airportwatch.org.uk/2021/10/government-puts-up-then-almost-instantly-withdraws-document-showing-need-for-behaviour-change-to-cut-carbon-emissions/(accessed 10 January 2022).

24　BEIS, 'Net Zero strategy: build back greener', October 2021, https://assets.publishing.service.gov.uk/government/uploads/system/uploads/attachment_data/file/1033990/net-zero-strategy-beis.pdf (accessed 10 January 2021).

Notes

Chapter 5

1 Interviewed by author (Zoom), 20 April 2021.
2 Planning Act 2008, s. 6 3(a).
3 Good Law Project, 'We have issued proceedings for judicial review', 23 May 2020, https://goodlawproject.org/news/judicial-review-energy-policy/ (accessed 10 January 2022).
4 *Vince et al. v Secretary of State for Business, Energy and Industrial Strategy et al.*, statement of facts and grounds.
5 'Drax scraps gas plant plans in Yorkshire, following climate concerns', edie.net, 25 February 2021, www.edie.net/news/6/Drax-scraps-gas-plant-plans-in-Yorkshire/ (accessed 10 January 2021).
6 Interviewed by author (phone), 8 April 2021.
7 Gwyn Topham, 'Carbon emissions from England's roads plan "100 times greater than government claims"', *The Guardian*, 6 April 2021, www.theguardian.com/environment/2021/apr/06/co2-from-englands-road-plan-up-to-100-times-more-than-dft-says (accessed 10 January 2022).
8 Gwyn Topham, '£27bn roads plan in doubt after Shapps overrode official advice', *The Guardian*, 10 January 2022, www.theguardian.com/uk-news/2021/feb/11/27bn-roads-plan-doubt-shapps-overrode-official-advice (accessed 10 January 2022).
9 Interviewed by author (phone), 8 April 2021.
10 Interviewed by author (Zoom), 20 December 2021.
11 Jenny Dawes, 'Support judicial review of Manston Airport DCO', Crowd Justice, www.crowdjustice.com/case/support-judicial-review-of-man/ (accessed 10 January 2022).
12 Veerle Heyvaert, 'Beware of populist narratives: the importance of getting the Heathrow ruling right', LSE blog, 29 February 2020, https://blogs.lse.ac.uk/politicsandpolicy/getting-the-heathrow-judgment-right/ (accessed 10 January 2022).
13 Interviewed by author (Zoom), 20 April 2021.
14 Heyvaert, 'Beware of populist narratives'.
15 Interviewed by author (in person), 18 October 2021.
16 Interviewed by author (phone), 20 December 2021.
17 Grantham Institute, 'Global trends in climate litigation'.
18 Interviewed by author (phone), 20 December 2021.
19 See www.lse.ac.uk/granthaminstitute/climate-change-laws-of-the-world-database/ (accessed 15 February 2021).

20 Speaking at Strathclyde conference 'Climate change legislation, lit-
    igation and the rule of law', Technology and Innovation Centre,
    Glasgow, 6 November 2021.
21 Ministry of Justice, 'Judicial review: proposals for reform', 13
    September 2021, https://consult.justice.gov.uk/judicial-review-
    reform/judicial-review-proposals-for-reform/ (accessed 10 January
    2021).
22 Editorial, '*The Guardian* view on judicial review: it's politics that
    needs fixing, not the courts', *The Guardian*, 19 March 2021, www.
    theguardian.com/commentisfree/2021/mar/19/the-guardian-
    view-on-judicial-review-its-politics-that-needs-fixing-not-the-courts
    (accessed 10 January 2022).
23 Suzanne Rab, 'Legal systems in the UK (England and Wales)',
    Thomson Reuters Practical Law, 1 March 2021, https://tmsnrt.
    rs/3zMb8Hs (accessed 10 January 2022).
24 Dominic Casciani, 'Right to challenge government in court over-
    hauled', BBC News, 18 March 2021, www.bbc.co.uk/news/uk-
    politics-56442162 (accessed 10 January 2022).
25 Joshua Rozenberg, 'Reviewing judicial review: how far will Raab
    go?', 17 October 2021, https://rozenberg.substack.com/p/review
    ing-judicial-review-d6d (accessed 10 January 2022).

Conclusion

 1 Kate Abnett, 'World heading for 2.4C warming after latest climate
    pledges', Reuters.com, 9 November 2021, www.reuters.com/business/
    cop/world-track-24c-global-warming-after-latest-pledges-analysts-
    2021-11-09/ (accessed 10 January 2022).
 2 Dan Whitehead, 'COVID-19: nearly 60% vow to fly less after get-
    ting coronavirus vaccination', Sky News, 22 April 2021, https://
    news.sky.com/story/covid-19-nearly-60-vow-to-fly-less-after-getting-
    coronavirus-vaccination-12283279 (accessed 10 January 2022).
 3 John Martin, 'Howard Davies: Heathrow Airport expansion "not
    needed at the moment"', City AM, 16 June 2021, www.cityam.com/
    howard-davies-heathrow-airport-expansion-not-needed-at-the-mo
    ment/ (accessed 10 January 2022).
 4 Bill Lehane, 'Spain's Ferrovial to halt funding for Heathrow: *Sunday
    Telegraph*', Bloomberg, 31 October 2021, www.bloomberg.com/news/

Notes

articles/2021-10-31/spain-s-ferrovial-to-halt-funding-for-heathrow-sunday-telegraph (accessed 10 January 2022).

5 Stefan Boscia, 'Extinction Rebellion patron buys stake in Heathrow Airport', City AM, 20 October 2019, www.cityam.com/extinction-rebellion-patron-buys-stake-in-heathrow-airport/ (accessed 10 January 2022).

6 Sandra Laville, 'Cleanup cost of Heathrow third runway doubles to £100bn, MPs told', *The Guardian*, 22 December 2021, www.theguardian.com/environment/2021/dec/22/cleanup-cost-of-heathrow-third-runway-doubles-to-100bn-mps-told (accessed 10 January 2022).

INDEX

Index

Index

Index